PRAYER:
Confronting the Confusion

Daniel Mann

PRAYER

Copyright © 2016 by Daniel Mann

Printed in the United States of America.

The Bible versions used in this publication are:

Mann, Daniel
Misheff, Van, editing

PRAYER:
Confronting the Confusion

SDG
ISBN-13: 978-0692747339 (Custom)
ISBN-10: 0692747338

PRAYER:
Confronting the Confusion

INTRODUCTION

This is not a how-to book. It is not about teaching prayer techniques or methods. Instead, it is about understanding prayer and, specifically, why our prayers are often not answered.

Prayer is—to define it as simply as possible—conversation with God. Therefore, a book should not be required to explain it. However, prayer can be a source of perplexity, doubt, and even discomfort. Consequently, this subject needs to be addressed.

Here are some of the questions and doubts that can arise concerning prayer:

- Do I have enough faith?
- Am I righteous enough?
- Am I asking in the right way?
- Does God love me enough to answer my prayers?
- Will my doubts prevent me
     from receiving anything from God?
- What does God expect from my prayers?
- Do I need to learn how to use my imagination?
- Are my thoughts getting in the way of my prayers?

In addition, there are currently a number of ideas gaining popular traction among Christians that have muddied the waters concerning prayer. In this book, I will confront those confusing teachings head-on.

My interest in this subject is so profound because for years I was afflicted with many of the doubts and questions I mentioned above. In fact, my uncertainties about prayer had reached the point where they were tormenting me. I therefore want my students and other Christians to experience the confidence that I now have as I pray. This new shift in my thinking came about as I began to understand what the Word has to say about God and prayer.

Prayer is a privilege. It can be a joyous experience. Moreover, it is vital to the Christian life. Even Jesus spent great lengths of time in prayer. Here are just two examples:

- One of those days Jesus went out to a mountainside to pray, and spent the night praying to God (Luke 6:12).

- After he had dismissed them, he went up on a mountainside by himself to pray. When evening came, he was there alone (Matthew 14:23).

These and many other accounts of Jesus praying should convince us that prayer is essential. I pray that this book will encourage Christians to engage in this precious privilege of communicating with the Almighty.

"If you remain in me and my words remain in you, ask whatever you wish, and it will be given you. This is to my Father's glory, that you bear much fruit, showing yourselves to be my disciples" (John 15:7-8).

Chapter 1

WHAT IS PRAYER?

People have different ideas about prayer. Some regard it as a mind-control exercise. Others regard prayer as a spiritual force, something we can learn to unleash. In <u>The Power of Prayer on Plants</u>, Rev. Franklin Loehr tries to make this very point:

- The discovery that prayer can measurably, and consistently, affect plant growth…is now recognized…Powers hitherto considered occult, extrasensory, or just plain magic, were given scientific proof…Man *does* have spiritual powers beyond his physical being (Loehr, Franklin. <u>The Power of Prayer on Plants</u>. Garden City, N.Y.: Doubleday, 1959:9).

Similarly, "Word of Faith" TV preacher Rod Parsley claims that prayer is a spiritual power that we must exercise if we want to receive anything from God:

- "When you ask God what He wants, He only tells you one time in the whole 1,166 pages of your Bible… 'Here's what I want: Ask of Me!' Why does He say that? Because He can't do it on His own. He can't get what He wants on His own because He placed you in authority on this earth. Did you hear me? He has to compel you to ask Him so that then He can answer, because He said, 'Call and I will answer' (Hunter, Robert, "Christianity Still in Crisis?" <u>Christian Research Journal</u> 30:3 (2007).

Thus, according to the so-called "Word of Faith" preachers, even God depends upon our spiritual authority!

This is so different from the teachings of Scripture. Jesus warned His disciples that we can do *nothing* apart from Him (John 15:5). Paul declared plainly our utter inadequacy. Instead, any competence we have in this area comes from God alone (2 Corinthians 3:5).

And yet, according to Parsley, God cannot answer our prayers "on His own" and is dependent on us to "…get what He wants." How preposterous! As we study the book of Job, however, we find that Job confessed the exact opposite of what Parsley is proposing. Take a look at what Job says as he addresses God Almighty:

- "I know that you can do everything, and that no purpose of yours can be withheld from you" (Job 42:2).

Did God correct Job's poor assessment of His authority? Not at all! Instead, God affirmed Job's words:

- After the LORD had said these things to Job, he said to Eliphaz the Temanite, "I am angry with you and your two friends, because you have not spoken of me what is right, as my servant Job has" (Job 42:7).

Why did God affirm Job? What had Job said that mattered so much to God? The answer is simple…Job had repented:

- "Therefore I despise myself and repent in dust and ashes" (Job 42:6).

This is so far removed from what some preachers are declaring today.

Let's look at another example of how someone from the pages of Scripture did NOT exercise their "spiritual authority," and yet God still orchestrated a most miraculous event.

Sarah certainly did not exercise her prayer power—according to Parsley and others of the same mind—when she overheard Yahweh promising Abraham a child. She was a ripe old 90 at the time and instead, she laughed at God's words in unbelief.

This prompted Yahweh to declare:

- "Is anything too hard for the LORD? At the appointed time I will return to you, according to the time of life, and Sarah shall have a son" (Genesis 18:14).

Evidently, Yahweh did not need to depend on Sarah to accomplish His purposes.

Nor did Jesus require Mary and Martha's prayers. They had sent word to Jesus to come heal their brother Lazarus, who was mortally ill. However, Jesus purposefully delayed coming at the time when their faith was at its peak—when Lazarus was sick but still alive. Instead, He allowed Lazarus to die and only arrived after he had been in the grave for four days. By this time, the sisters had given up all hope and had even stopped praying.

Here is what happened when Jesus finally arrived:

- "Lord," Martha said to Jesus, "if you had been here, my brother would not have died. But I know that even now God will give you whatever you ask." Jesus said to her, "Your brother will rise again." Martha answered, "I know he will rise again in the resurrection at the last day" (John 11:21-24).

While it seemed that Martha did have faith that Jesus could raise up her brother, she only thought that this was possible as part of the future general resurrection. In her conversation with the Lord, she was hedging her bets. However, Jesus proved most decisively that He had no need of her faith or her prayers. As we all know—and despite her lack of faith—Jesus went on to raise Martha's brother from the dead!

Once again…what is prayer, and how does God desire us to pray?

Clearly, it's not about the exercise of certain techniques or powers. It's not about controlling our brain waves or even our thinking. Prayer is about something more fundamental and relational.

We know that the Roman centurion Cornelius was heard by God. But why?

- He and all his family were devout and God-fearing; he gave generously to those in need and prayed to God regularly (Acts 10:2).

Cornelius and his family were "God-fearing." God was first in their lives. Cornelius "gave generously to those in need and prayed to God regularly." God sent an angel to him, announcing:

- "Your prayers and gifts to the poor have come up as a memorial offering before God" (Acts 10:4).

Our Lord therefore sent the apostle Peter to preach the Gospel to Cornelius and his relatives. As the whole family listened, God filled them with the Holy Spirit. There is no mention here or in any other place in the Bible that they first had to learn a set of prayer techniques or master any aids for improving concentration.

In contrast with the biblical revelation, the Quaker mystic Richard Foster teaches that if we want to receive anything from God, we must exercise our imagination. Let us see what

Foster had to say as he was coaching parents about how to pray for their children:

- Imagine the light of Christ flowing through your hands and healing every emotional trauma and hurt feeling your child experienced that day. Fill him or her with the peace and joy of the Lord. In sleep the child is very receptive to prayer since the conscious mind, which tends to erect barriers to God's gentle influence, is relaxed (Foster, Richard. Celebration of Discipline. New York: HarperCollins, 1980: 39).

So, according to this line of thinking, if our creativity is lacking, and we are not able to imagine or envision "the light of Christ flowing" through our hands, we are sunk. Our prayers have little hope of being answered.

However, Scripture never identifies any lack of exercising our imagination as a reason for the failure of our prayers. Instead, Scripture consistently identifies our hard heart towards God as the problem. The Lord explained this clearly to His prophet, Zechariah:

- "But they refused to pay attention; stubbornly they turned their backs and stopped up their ears. They made their hearts as hard as flint and would not listen to the law or to the words that the LORD Almighty had sent by his Spirit through the earlier prophets. So the LORD Almighty was very angry. 'When I called, they did not listen; so when they called, I would not listen,' says the LORD Almighty" (Zechariah 7:11-13).

Israel's problem was not that they had failed to exercise their imagination, but that they had turned away from the Lord.

Prayer isn't magical; nor is it a secret power or even a skill. Instead, it is a matter of being real with God (Psalm 51:6). Our words must express truth and sincerity. Our prayers are not heard because they are insincere. The Lord explained this as He spoke to Jeremiah about the idolatry and hypocrisy of Judah:

- "…'From the time I brought your forefathers up from Egypt until today, I warned them again and again, saying, "Obey me." But they did not listen or pay attention; instead, they followed the stubbornness of their evil hearts'…Therefore this is what the LORD says: 'I will bring on them a disaster they cannot escape. Although they cry out to me, I will not listen to them. The towns of Judah and the people of Jerusalem will go and cry out to the gods to whom they burn incense, but they will not help them at all when disaster strikes. You have as many gods as you have towns, O Judah; and the altars you have set up to burn incense to that shameful god Baal are as many as the streets of Jerusalem.' Do not pray for this people nor offer any plea or petition for them, because I will not listen when they call to me in the time of their distress" (Jeremiah 11:7-8a, 11-14).

Only the Sovereign Lord could rescue Judah—not their gods or their various means of petitioning God or even the prayers of Jeremiah. They had violated God's covenant and had *refused* to return. They had turned their backs on God, and now He would turn His back on them.

When Israel turned their back on the Lord, they also turned their back on the commandments of the Lord. Therefore, when the Lord charged the tribe of Judah with unfaithfulness to their wives, He was also charging them with unfaithfulness to Him and even to the commandments He had given them:

- Another thing you do: You flood the LORD's altar with tears. You weep and wail because he no longer pays attention to your offerings or accepts them with pleasure from your hands. You ask, "Why?" It is because the LORD is acting as the witness between you and the wife of your youth, because you have broken faith with her, though she is your partner, the wife of your marriage covenant (Malachi 2:13-14).

Judah wondered why God wasn't responding to their offerings and sacrifices, or even to their cries and tears. If they weren't living sincerely and obediently—a yardstick of their faithfulness—all of their fervency was for naught.

The men of Judah had not been faithful with their wives. And what is more, they were making no effort to correct the matter. It would be impossible for mere tears to rectify this grievous situation. Moreover, the attainment of any sort of "state of relaxation" would have had absolutely no effect on God changing His mind.

Only sincere confession of our sins and repentance can bring about healing in our relationship with God!

There are some people who are under the strong delusion that *they* can atone for their own sins. They endeavor to do this by punishing or even cutting themselves, believing that they will gain some sort of merit or standing before God for their actions. However, even these acts of intense self-punishment will always fail to engage God.

Consider the wrong-headed thinking of the man who beats up his wife and then—in what he considers an act of great self-punishment or sacrifice—takes her on an expensive vacation. This kind of behavior in no way replaces the need for him to humbly confess his sins and demonstrate in a very tangible way that he is truly repentant. God requires no less from us!

Peter echoes the same truth. When we give our sins safe haven by not confessing and repenting, we build a wall against God:

- Husbands, in the same way be considerate as you live with your wives, and treat them with respect as the weaker partner and as heirs with you of the gracious gift of life, so that nothing will hinder your prayers. Finally, all of you, live in harmony with one another; be sympathetic, love as brothers, be compassionate and humble. Do not repay evil with evil or insult with insult, but with blessing, because to this you were called so that you may inherit a blessing. For, "Whoever would love life and see good days must keep his tongue from evil and his lips from deceitful speech. He must turn from evil and do good; he must seek peace and pursue it. *For the eyes of the Lord are on the righteous and his ears are attentive to their prayer, but the face of the Lord is against those who do evil*" (1 Peter 3:7-12, emphasis added).

When we refuse His will, His teachings, and the righteous life He expects of us, we also refuse Him. In effect, we are telling Him, "I can live my life just fine without Your meddling...I don't need You to answer my prayers."

What does it mean to be righteous? Does it mean that we have to achieve a certain level of spiritual perfection? This is an important question, because Scripture tells us that God is attentive to the righteous (Psalm 4:3; Proverbs 15:29). We must always keep in mind that the righteous are not morally perfect—none of us are! *The righteous are those who turn from their sins*:

- Turn from evil and do good; seek peace and pursue it. The eyes of the LORD are on the righteous [those who turn from evil] and his ears are attentive to their cry; the face of the LORD is against those who do evil, to cut off the memory of them from the earth. The righteous cry out, and the LORD hears them; he delivers them from all their troubles. The LORD is close to the brokenhearted and saves those who are crushed in spirit. A righteous man may have many troubles, but the LORD delivers him from them all (Psalm 34:14-19).

Strikingly, King David counted himself among the righteous, even after his adultery with Bathsheba and the murder of her husband, Uriah (Psalm 32). David had been assured that God had forgiven him, and that had made all the difference!

Prayer is not a matter of magic or of gimmickry, but rather a sincere and humble cry to a loving, heavenly Father who is able and most willing to lift us up and wash us off.

Chapter 2

FERVENT PRAYER

The Apostle James wrote that the "effectual fervent prayer of a righteous man availeth much" (James 5:16, KJV). So then, how is it that we can pray fervently? Is it simply a matter of generating emotion when we pray? Not at all! We might have been able to manipulate our mothers with our emotional outbursts, but not God. I do not think that there is one verse in the Bible that even suggests that God will respond to us simply because we are able to produce a certain quota of tears.

Esau shed many tears when he realized that he had been deprived of his father Isaac's blessing. However, his crying made no difference to the Lord. After all, his tears were *not* accompanied by repentance and the genuine confession of his sins:

- See that no one is sexually immoral, or is godless like Esau, who for a single meal sold his inheritance rights as the oldest son. Afterward, as you know, when he wanted to inherit this blessing, he was rejected. He could bring about no change of mind, though he sought the blessing with tears (Hebrews 12:16-17).

It was the very same way with Judas Iscariot, who betrayed Jesus and felt guilty for what he had done. In a desperate show of emotion, he threw back the 30 pieces of silver to those who had bought his betrayal and went out and hung himself (Matthew 27:3-10). Even his guilt, desperation and suicide failed to incline heaven in his direction (John 17:12). He had rejected Jesus' Gospel and failed to humble himself before the Lord by confessing his sins. Instead, he insisted on atoning for his sins on his own terms and in his own way.

Now, let us examine one of the episodes in the life of Ahab, one of the worst of the kings of Israel:

- There was never a man like Ahab, who sold himself to do evil in the eyes of the LORD...He behaved in the vilest manner by going after idols, like the Amorites...(1 Kings 21:25-26a).

However, in desperation, this wicked king humbled himself before the Lord after a prophet had announced his impending death:

- When Ahab heard these words, he tore his clothes, put on sackcloth and fasted. He lay in sackcloth and went around meekly. Then the word of the LORD came to Elijah the Tishbite: "Have you noticed how Ahab has humbled himself before me? Because he has humbled himself, I will not bring this disaster in his day, but I will bring it on his house in the days of his son" (1 Kings 21:27-29).

This account does not mention either "confession" or "repentance." However, his behavior before the Lord and the Lord's response indicate that Ahab had been genuinely repentant. Moreover, the fact that Ahab had "humbled himself" strongly suggests that he had confessed his sins to the Lord. Even though we know that Ahab returned to his old shenanigans a few years later, it is clear that in this instance God indeed responded favorably to the way that this king humbled himself.

One of the kings of Judah, Manasseh, was even more evil than Ahab. However, in desperation, after he had been thrown into prison by the Babylonians, he cried out to God, who forgave him:

Confronting the Confusion

- In his distress he sought the favor of the LORD his God and humbled himself greatly before the God of his fathers. And when he prayed to him, the LORD was moved by his entreaty and listened to his plea; so he brought him back to Jerusalem and to his kingdom (2 Chronicles 33:12-13).

What made the difference in the case of these two kings? Desperately trying to save their lives, both kings humbled themselves, which always involves a confession of sins.

However, fervent prayer does not always need to depend on an immediate threat to our lives. Instead, our fervency in prayer can grow exponentially when we come to the point of despairing of ourselves.

Yes, you heard me right. Now let me explain…

It is a comfort for most of us to trust in and have a high estimation of ourselves, of our performance and ability to handle any situation. This is our natural default. Why is this so true? Well, it is this self-confidence that gets us out of bed in the morning. It enables us to confront life and to take risks. Without it, we would obsessively and painfully turn inward. Some psychologists even believe that a certain degree of self-delusion is necessary in order for us to attain an empowering self-esteem.

And yet, we will never learn "God-trust" as long as we remain addicted to self-trust. As long as we feel that we can handle life, prayer will only feel like an unnecessary encumbrance—something we might feel obligated to perform out of a sense of duty. As a consequence, prayer—looked at this way—will begin to feel more and more like a burden. We will find ourselves praying less and less.

Even the Apostle Paul admitted that he had to learn *not* to trust in himself. Only then could he truly trust in God:

- We do not want you to be uninformed, brothers, about the hardships we suffered in the province of Asia. We were under great pressure, far beyond our ability to endure, so that we despaired even of life. Indeed, in our hearts we felt the sentence of death. But this happened that we might not rely on ourselves but on God, who raises the dead. He has delivered us from such a deadly peril, and he will deliver us. On him we have set our hope that he will continue to deliver us... (2 Corinthians 1:8-10).

God brought Paul to the limits of his ability to cope with life. In desperation, he had only one other hope—God. This is a lesson that I must repeatedly learn. When life is going well, I tend to feel good about myself and my abilities. However, He has shown me that my cockiness is merely setting the stage for my fall.

In my early years as a believer, I was troubled by a verse that declared that the normal Christian is characterized by an intense love for God:

- In this [salvation] you greatly rejoice, though now for a little while you may have had to suffer grief in all kinds of trials. These have come so that your faith—of greater worth than gold, which perishes even though refined by fire—may be proved genuine and may result in praise, glory and honor when Jesus Christ is revealed. Though you have not seen him, you love him; and even though you do not see him now, you believe in him and are filled with an inexpressible and glorious joy (1 Peter 1:6-8).

Did I really love Him? Was I "filled with an inexpressible and glorious joy?" I had serious doubts. It was painful for me to realize that, for some reason, I seemed to be spiritually deficient. To further add to my woes, I began to wonder…is God withholding Himself from me? Could it be that He likes me less than others? My thoughts and questions began to torment me.

However, as I endured years of suffering and despaired of my own ability to shoulder the burden of this life called "Daniel," I had no choice other than to trust in Him. Was I courageous? Was I long-suffering? Absolutely not! There was simply no one else to whom I could turn. He was patiently refining my faith by killing the former object of my faith—me—so that my hope would rest exclusively and totally in Him.

When all my self-esteem was revealed and then taken away, He became all that I truly had. Only He stood between me and psychological melt-down. Before this paradigm shift in my thinking, I had regarded Him as simply my Helper when things got tough. However, after life became so difficult as to be unbearable, He became my Lover and Savior. Now it is easier for me to understand and truly appreciate what Peter said about the relationship that we can have with our Savior: "…you believe in him and are filled with an inexpressible and glorious joy." When we see that He is all we have, we can also see that He is all we need. As the Psalmist wrote:

- Whom have I in heaven but you? And earth has nothing I desire besides you. My flesh and my heart may fail, but God is the strength of my heart and my portion forever (Psalm 73:25-26).

As God lovingly breaks us of any dependence on ourselves, these verses become increasingly real for us. However, this cannot happen without a regular diet of suffering:

- Dear friends, do not be surprised at the painful trial you are suffering, as though something strange were happening to you. But rejoice that you participate in the sufferings of Christ, so that you may be overjoyed when his glory is revealed (1 Peter 4:12-13).

How does this take place? How are we to love Him and to be "overjoyed when his glory is revealed?" This will only happen after we utterly despair of all the other possible "saviors," especially the savior that leads the pack—ourselves. It is only then that our hope will be centered squarely on our Messiah and on His glorious return.

The Jews of Jabesh Gilead had become terribly desperate. They had despaired of their ability to defend themselves against the Ammonite King Nahash. In fact, they were so desperate that they even offered themselves to the king as slaves. However, this was not good enough for Nahash:

- But Nahash the Ammonite replied, "I will make a treaty with you only on the condition that I gouge out the right eye of every one of you and so bring disgrace on all Israel" (1 Samuel 11:2).

The reluctant Saul had just recently been appointed as King of Israel. The Jews of Jabesh Gilead sent him their frantic plea for help. It was the longest of long-shots. However:

- When Saul heard their words, the Spirit of God came upon him in power, and he burned with anger (1 Samuel 11:6).

Saul defeated the Ammonites, and the Jews were delivered. For forty years, they remained grateful to Saul. When they heard that he had been killed in battle by the Philistines, the men of Jabesh Gilead made a long and perilous journey to recover his body and give the king a proper burial.

We too need to learn how to be grateful.

But we will never learn this valuable trait as long as we are under the illusion that we can handle our own lives. We have to come to the point of utter despair, like the Jews of Jabesh. We must learn to be grateful and to regard prayer as our only lifeline. It is essential for us to realize that without our Savior, we can do nothing (John 15:5). We are helpless sheep without a shepherd. When we learn this wonderful truth, our prayers will display a fervency which they could never ordinarily have.

However, this does not mean that God will not hear us until we reach a certain level of spiritual maturity. On the contrary, Scripture warns us that we don't even know how to pray or what to pray for. But that is totally beside the point. It simply does not matter! For here, as in every other area of our lives, God has us covered. It is the Holy Spirit Himself Who prays fervently for us:

- In the same way, the Spirit helps us in our weakness. We do not know what we ought to pray for, but the Spirit himself intercedes for us with groans that words cannot express. And he who searches our hearts knows the mind of the Spirit, because the Spirit intercedes for the saints in accordance with God's will (Romans 8:26-27).

May His Holy Name be praised forever and ever!

Chapter 3

GOD'S INCREDIBLE GRACE

We are all highly sinful and unworthy of God, and we sense our unworthiness. Therefore, we tend to obsess and doubt:

- Do I have enough faith to receive anything from the Lord? Many of my prayers haven't been answered. Perhaps God didn't answer my prayer about saving me? Perhaps I doubt too much? Does He love me enough to answer my prayers?

One young man wondered whether he was worthy enough to be saved. Terrified at the prospect of going to hell, he took a radical step. He forfeited everything he had to become an Augustinian monk. He had been taught that this was the surest way to please God and to merit salvation. However, even after this radical move, he remained tortured by doubts and thoughts of eternal torment.

He subjected himself to the most extreme deprivations, along with four hours of daily confessions, but nothing relieved him. Finally, his vicar advised him:

- Luther, all you need to do is just love God!

To this, Martin Luther bellowed back, "Love Him? I hate Him!" He later wrote that He could not love God if he could not be sure that God loved him back and would receive him into heaven. However, years later, while preparing a lesson on Paul's letter to the Roman church, Luther encountered a verse that would change his life: "And the just shall live by faith" (Romans 1:17). He suddenly realized that he didn't have to earn God's love. Instead, it was there waiting for him. He just needed to receive it in faith.

Luther later wrote that it felt as if the gates of heaven had opened for him. He was then enabled to trust that God loved him.

Let me guess what you are thinking right now:

- This certainty of God's love is miles away from me. Sometimes I wonder whether assurance like this is even possible for someone like me, who doubts and questions.

Certainly, there are many reasons to doubt and question. The Bible gives multiple assurances that God is love, but there are also a number of verses that make it seem like His love is conditional, that we are being required to fulfill a set of impossible stipulations. Take, for instance, Hebrews 12:14:

- Make every effort to live in peace with all men and to be holy; without holiness no one will see the Lord.

This verse, among others, is guaranteed to be a doubt-maker for some believers…

- How holy must I be? It doesn't seem that any of my thoughts, motives or deeds are entirely holy. They are all sin-infested. Is there a certain level of holiness that I must attain before I can be saved? Isn't the Bible therefore a collection of contradictions?

Can we truly be confident of the grace of God when these questions remain unanswered? Not entirely. Consequently, I think that we need to take a deeper look at Scripture.

Jesus' actions didn't often look like love. He continually criticized His own disciples. At times, it seemed that they couldn't do anything right. He commended faith only twice in Scripture, and on both occasions it was the faith of Gentiles—

the Canaanite woman (Matthew 15:28) and the Roman Centurion (Matthew 8:10). He never commended the faith of His disciples. He never told them anything like this:

- You men are really first class. Choosing you was the best thing I have ever done. You are such quick learners and, oh, so spiritual!

Jesus never encouraged His disciples. Is this the way to win and sustain a following? Rather than building confidence in the heavenly destiny of His followers, many of Jesus' teachings served to undermine their confidence. However, after His final discourse with His disciples, Jesus prayed to the Father. This prayer illuminates a different perspective—a heavenly one! And this makes perfect sense because Jesus is no longer addressing His disciples, but His Father:

- "I have revealed you to those whom you gave me out of the world. They were yours; you gave them to me and *they have obeyed your word.* Now they know that everything you have given me comes from you. For I gave them the words you gave me and *they accepted them. They knew with certainty that I came from you, and they believed that you sent me*" (John 17:6-8, emphasis added).

Perhaps you've read these verses too often to notice their transcendent perspective. These words do not represent Jesus' usual words of censure like, "Get behind me Satan" (Matthew 16:23) or, "Could you men not keep watch with me for one hour?" (Matthew 26:40)

Instead, Jesus' words are other-worldly. About His fumbling disciples, Jesus prays, "…they have obeyed your word…they accepted [the words you gave me]…They knew with certainty that I came from you, and they believed that you sent me."

24

These words are astounding and yet perplexing at the same time. From our earthly perspective, the disciples didn't even understand His Word, let alone obey it!

To illustrate this point, I will quote five statements made by the disciples prior to Jesus praying from His heavenly perspective in John 17. All of these words demonstrate their lack of understanding:

- Thomas said to him, "Lord, we don't know where you are going, so how can we know the way?" (John 14:5)

- Philip said, "Lord, show us the Father and that will be enough for us" (John 14:8).

The disciples were totally unaware that *they had already seen the Father*, in Jesus.

- Then Judas (not Judas Iscariot) said, "But, Lord, why do you intend to show yourself to us and not to the world?" (John 14:22)

- Some of his disciples said to one another, "What does he mean by saying, 'In a little while you will see me no more, and then after a little while you will see me,' and 'Because I am going to the Father'?" They kept asking, "What does he mean by 'a little while'? We don't understand what he is saying" (John 16:17-18).

- Then Jesus' disciples said, "Now you are speaking clearly and without figures of speech. Now we can see that you know all things and that you do not even need to have anyone ask you questions. This makes us believe that you came from God" (John 16:29-30).

Before you commend the disciples for what they said in the last statement, keep in mind that, at this point, they were just about ready to disown their faith!

These ignorant statements weren't unusual for the Apostles. They often seemed clueless about their Master, and Jesus wasn't hesitant to let them know this. However, when Jesus talked to His Father, we recognize a different perspective. From these heights, we are invited to view an entirely different landscape. We learn that the disciples are to be commended to the Father because "they have obeyed your word"!

This is the gracious heavenly reality.

You might think that this distinction between the earthly viewpoint and the heavenly one is just a weird anomaly. However, this same distinction is found throughout Scripture.

Let me offer just a few examples...

The prophet-for-hire Balaam had also been granted a view from this same mountain-top. He had been hired by the King of Moab, Balak, to curse Israel. However, God had warned Balaam to say only what He would reveal to him. God had opened his eyes so that he could penetrate the haze and see reality from the perspective of God. And this is what he saw:

- The oracle of one who hears the words of God, who sees a vision from the Almighty, who falls prostrate, and whose eyes are opened: "How beautiful are your tents, O Jacob, your dwelling places, O Israel!" (Numbers 24:4-5)

- "He has not observed iniquity in Jacob, nor has He seen wickedness in Israel. The LORD his God is with him, and the shout of a King is among them" (Numbers 23:21).

There was probably little that was "beautiful" about Jacob's tents, especially after wandering 40 years in the desert. Balaam was beholding a transcendent reality. Clearly, there was *gross* "iniquity in Jacob" and no shortage of "wickedness in Israel," but this is not what God was seeing! He sees a different reality, a reality that transcends our own. He sees the end from the beginning.

Likewise in the New Testament, God shows us a vision of the Apostles and servants of Christ in a most glorious setting:

- And God raised us up with Christ and seated us with him in the heavenly realms in Christ Jesus… (Ephesians 2:6).

In the eyes of the Lord, our status is dramatically transformed when we turn from our sins. When we repent, we are transported into the kingdom of His beloved Son, where we sit "in the heavenly realms in Christ Jesus." We become His vessels of glory.

Job had made many rash indictments against God during his lengthy trial. However, it was not upon Job, but upon his three friends that God brought damning charges:

- "I am angry with you and your two friends, because you have not spoken of me what is right, as my servant Job has. So now take seven bulls and seven rams and go to my servant Job and sacrifice a burnt offering for yourselves. My servant Job will pray for you, and I will accept his prayer and not deal with you according to your folly. You have not spoken of me what is right, as my servant Job has" (Job 42:7-8).

This is peculiar for many reasons. For one thing, Job seemed to have talked far worse about God than had his three friends. Second of all, God—against the evidence to the contrary—

said that Job had spoken correctly of Him! Clearly, this wasn't accurate...or was it? From God's heavenly perspective, Job had just repented twice of his rash words (Job 42:6; 40:4-5), and all had been forgiven. According to 1 John 1:9, when we confess our sins and repent, we are not only forgiven, we are cleansed of all unrighteousness.

And that had made all the difference in the world to God...and Job!

We must remember that God's heavenly perspective transcends the temporal. His perspective trumps all of our failures and sins in this world. Once again, God does not see as we do. While He is not blind to the earthly, He sees a high and eternal reality—a reality in which everything is wiped clean, where love and righteousness remove from sight everything that makes us cringe in shame.

Let's take a look at some more examples where we can see this truth on display...

Lot lived in Sodom and willingly partook in its life. When the two angels showed up to investigate Sodom's sinfulness, Lot hurriedly rushed them off to his home, hoping to dispatch them early in the morning, without consequence to his town.

Every step of Lot's life had been soiled by compromise. He even got drunk and had sex with his two daughters. However, this isn't the final word about Lot. In the New Testament, we find that, in God's eyes, Lot was regarded in an entirely different light. 2 Peter 2:7 declares that Lot was "a righteous man."

The Bible speaks of two distinct realities. According to the first reality, we have all fallen short of God's standards (Romans 3:23) and deserve condemnation (Romans 6:23). However, there is another reality that eclipses the first one. It is a reality where "Mercy triumphs over judgment," according to James 2:13. It is a reality where we are new creations in Christ. We are children of the light, and according to Romans 10:13, anyone who calls upon God shall be saved!

What can we learn from the life of Abraham, "the father of us all," as it is written in Romans 4:16? From a human perspective, Abraham had been a spiritual failure. He continually doubted God's promises. Even after Yahweh appeared and assured him that Sarah would give birth to the promised son in the following year, Abraham once again wimped out and passed off his beloved wife as his sister.

Consequently the local king, ignorant of the truth of the matter, grabbed Sarah for his harem. However, before he could have sex with her, God struck down the entire nation of Gerar with a disease. He then appeared to the king in a dream and instructed him to return Sarah to her husband Abraham.

The shocked king then confronted Abraham about his deception. Abraham admitted his cowardice:

- "I said to myself, 'There is surely no fear of God in this place, and they will kill me because of my wife.' ...And when God had me wander from my father's household, I said to her, 'This is how you can show your love to me: Everywhere we go, say of me, "He is my brother"'" (Genesis 20:11-13).

Abraham's unfaithfulness had a long history. In spite of this, when God appeared to the king in a dream, He uttered some of the most profound words in all of Scripture:

- "Now return the man's wife, for he is a prophet, and he will pray for you and you will live. But if you do not return her, you may be sure that you and all yours will die" (Genesis 20:7).

Even after Abraham had disgraced God so thoroughly, God remained faithful. Despite his failings, Abraham remained His "prophet." And, besides all this, the king was forced to depend upon the cowardly failure Abraham to pray for him!

The king might have thought, "What kind of God chooses such low-life as prophets like this?" However, God's love and protection for his failing prophet did not falter. In fact, Abraham is esteemed by God in this incredibly gracious way:

- Against all hope, Abraham in hope believed and so became the father of many nations, just as it had been said to him, "So shall your offspring be." Without weakening in his faith, he faced the fact that his body was as good as dead—since he was about a hundred years old—and that Sarah's womb was also dead. Yet he did not waver through unbelief regarding the promise of God, but was strengthened in his faith and gave glory to God, being fully persuaded that God had power to do what he had promised (Romans 4:18-21).

Once again, God does not see as we see. He sees us from His perspective—through gracious and loving eyes.

We often fear that we lack enough faith to be saved. Hebrews 11, known as the "hall of fame of faith," gives us unbelievable portraits of exemplary faith. But if we read closely, we will be shocked at what we find. This chapter of Hebrews tells us that by faith, "Abraham was enabled to become a father" (Hebrews 11:11). However, as we recall the story from Genesis, it doesn't seem that Abraham had much faith at all.

We are also told that "By faith [Moses] left Egypt, not fearing the king's anger (Hebrews 11:27). However, the original account tells us that Moses did fear!

My favorite example of faith regards the children of Israel:

- By faith the people passed through the Red Sea as on dry land; but when the Egyptians tried to do so, they were drowned (Hebrews 11:29).

This is incredible! Israel was anything but a model of faith. The original Exodus account tells us that the Israelites rebelled against Moses as soon as they heard the Egyptian chariots approaching!

From an earthly perspective, Israel was a sorry mess, but not from God's gracious perspective. Here is another glimpse into His thinking:

- But God demonstrates his own love for us in this: While we were still sinners, Christ died for us. Since we have now been justified by his blood, how much more shall we be saved from God's wrath through him! For if, when we were God's enemies, we were reconciled to him through the death of his Son, how much more, having been reconciled, shall we be saved through his life! (Romans 5:8-10)

God's logic is both illuminating and persuasive. If He was willing to pay the supreme price for us, when we were yet sinners—His enemies—wouldn't He protect His investment now that we have been made His friends?

Perhaps an analogy might help...

If you go to the junk-yard and purchase a rusted-out Model-T Ford for an exorbitant price, and then spend the next several years restoring it to its original form, would you then discard it? Certainly not! You would now treasure it and do whatever you could to preserve it.

Our Lord paid the absolute highest price for the sins of all of humanity. As a consequence, any member of the human race who comes to Him, He will in no way cast out (John 6:37). After all, why would he do such a thing? He's already paid the ultimate price for us!

God even pursues those who refuse Him...

He pursued David, His King. David deserved only the worst from God. God had given David everything, but this didn't satisfy him. He saw a woman he wanted and he took her, even though she was already married. Not only that, but David even had Bathsheba's husband killed to cover up his sin.

However, God was not going to be mocked. Sin would require a price. Despite David's many prayers, God took Bathsheba's newborn baby. However, she conceived again, and David named his child "Solomon." In Hebrew, Solomon is "Shlomo," a form of "Shalom," meaning peace. It seems that David was hoping that this child would represent peace between God and him. But how could David expect anything good from such a sin-stained relationship?

However, God had another name in mind:

- Then David comforted his wife Bathsheba, and he went to her and lay with her. She gave birth to a son, and they named him Solomon. The Lord loved him; and because the Lord loved him, he sent word through Nathan the prophet to name him Jedidiah (2 Samuel 12:24-25).

David hadn't been hopeful enough!

Instead of Solomon being a mere "peace" child, he was "Jedidiah," meaning, "Beloved of God." From an earthly perspective, David and his new wife didn't deserve anything but punishment from God. However, God heard David's prayer, forgave his sin, and cleansed the entire relationship.

On top of this, out of all of David's sons, God chose *Solomon* to become the next king of Israel. God can salvage even the worst of lives and relationships!

And now, what can we learn from the Apostle to the Gentiles?

Paul, having hardened his heart, was even God's persecutor. Not only did he kill Christians, but He also forced them to blaspheme Jesus. I cannot think of anything worse. However, Paul explained:

- Christ Jesus came into the world to save sinners—of whom I am the worst. But for that very reason I was shown mercy so that in me, the worst of sinners, Christ Jesus might display his unlimited patience as an example for those who would believe on him and receive eternal life (1 Timothy 1:15-16).

Paul served as an example of God's readiness to extend His forgiveness to anyone, including the worst sinners. If God was willing to forgive Paul, He would be willing to forgive anyone who would come to Him!

King Manasseh was another example of God's incredible mercy. He was the worst of the worst. He reigned for 55 years in Jerusalem and bathed the city with the blood of the righteous. Scripture informs us that he was worse than the Canaanites. However, even Manasseh found the mercy of God when he repented of his sins (2 Chronicles 33:10-13).

The meaning is clear. If God forgave and restored Manasseh, the worst of the worst, He would certainly respond favorably to anyone who would call upon His name!

Let me again guess what you are thinking:

- Well, you make salvation seem as if it's available to anyone who confesses their sins. But how about that verse you cited before which says, "...without holiness no one will see the Lord"? I don't think that I can be holy enough.

Let's take a look at how the book of Hebrews illustrates what holiness means, through the example of Esau:

- [See to it] lest there be any fornicator or profane person like Esau, who for one morsel of food sold his birthright. For you know that afterward, when he wanted to inherit the blessing, he was rejected, for he found no place for repentance, though he sought it [the blessing] diligently with tears (Hebrews 12:16-17, NKJV).

Esau wasn't rejected because of his sins—we are all sinners. He was rejected *because he was unwilling to repent* that he had sold his birthright for a bowl of soup, demonstrating that he did not esteem the things of God. Although he wept over losing his father's blessing, the things of God were foolishness to him.

Now that we have taken a look at a number of examples from the Bible, I wonder...how does God regard *us*? We lack the superlatives to answer this question.

Paul wrote of the love of God this way:

- I pray that you, being rooted and established in love, may have power, together with all the saints, to grasp how wide and long and high and deep is the love of Christ, and to know this love that surpasses knowledge—that you may be filled to the measure of all the fullness of God (Ephesians 3:17-19).

34

God's love for us is a love that "surpasses knowledge." Why then can't we see this? Why does our God obscure this glorious reality, causing us to walk in uncertainty? Perhaps we are not ready for the light.

As Jesus told His disciples, there were certain truths that would not yet be good for them to see:

- "I have much more to say to you, more than you can now bear" (John 16:12).

We as well cannot bear to behold the beauty of the tents of Israel and certainly not our own glory. I think that it was C.S. Lewis who said that if we could see our glory, we would worship each other.

However, sometimes God does open our eyes to glimpse this transcendent reality. For example, Paul claims that for those who are being saved, "we are…the [sweet] aroma of Christ" (2 Corinthians 2:15). This is amazing! How can we, with all of our spiritual warts, manifest as the aroma of Christ?

Although God does allow us a glimpse of His reality from time to time, we cannot handle this light in sustained doses. We lack the mental maturity to assimilate this knowledge in a profitable way. In the midst of a life-threatening chain saw injury, I was lying in a pool of blood, thinking that this breath would be my last. Suddenly, I realized that I was not alone. I was so overcome by the presence of God that I was in ecstasy. I knew that even if I died, God would be there with me, and that I was totally safe and loved by Him.

I was miraculously rescued and spent the next four days recuperating in the hospital. On the second day, my surgeon warned that I would have to exercise my half-cut-off wrist or lose its functionality. However, after my divine encounter, I was convinced that the God who had saved me was great enough to restore my hand without any exercises. Consequently, I did not exercise my hand…and it was not restored as it might have been.

My theology—my understanding—did not measure up to what God had revealed to me. I had wrongly thought that since God is omnipotent, I did not have to do anything. Now I understand that, although God is all-powerful, this doesn't relieve me of my earthly responsibilities.

Perhaps even after imbibing all of these verses, you are still left with uncertainty about God's love and your salvation. That's certainly not unusual. Sometimes, even knowledge of the Word will not take us everywhere we would like to go, nor should it. God has not constructed our lives so that we would make ourselves self-sufficient through wisdom. Instead, we are always to depend upon lowly, humble prayer. In this kind of prayer, we acknowledge that we and our wisdom are not enough. We need *His* intervention.

And He will intervene!

When we ask our Lord for assurance about His love and our salvation, we are asking according to His will. Therefore, we can be confident that *He will answer.*

Chapter 4

GREAT FAITH

We tend to think of great faith in terms of quantity. So did Jesus' disciples. They asked Him to "increase our faith" (Luke 17:5). That was the wrong request, and so Jesus told them a little parable:

- He replied, "If you have faith as small as a mustard seed, you can say to this mulberry tree, 'Be uprooted and planted in the sea,' and it will obey you" (Luke 17:6).

Quantity wasn't the issue. Even if the disciples had the smallest measure of faith—a mustard seed's worth—they could move forests. Instead, faith was about *quality*, as shown in Jesus' next parable, which concluded:

- "So you also, when you have done everything you were told to do, should say, 'We are unworthy servants; we have only done our duty'" (Luke 17:10).

A mature faith involves an understanding of the truth about God and us. Even the most productive and spiritual among us should regard themselves as "unworthy servants," as totally underserving of *anything* from God, even a "thank you." We must remember that anything good that we receive from God is totally a matter of His grace.

Jesus presented many teachings about how faith and prayer should include this humble understanding:

- To some who were confident of their own righteousness and looked down on everybody else, Jesus told this parable (Luke 18:9).

Jesus presented two people for His disciples to consider. The first one was a Pharisee who trusted that he was righteous and deserving:

- "The Pharisee stood up and prayed *about himself*: 'God, I thank you that I am not like other men—robbers, evildoers, adulterers—or even like this tax collector'" (Luke 18:11, emphasis added).

The Pharisee's prayer was rejected by God. It was totally self-centered, with a spotlight on his accomplishments.

In contrast, the other person acknowledged that he was a sinner and didn't deserve anything from God. Jesus concluded that since this man humbled himself to acknowledge the truth—that he was a sinner—his prayer was received:

- "I tell you that this man, rather than the other, went home justified before God. For everyone who exalts himself will be humbled, and he who humbles himself will be exalted" (Luke 18:14).

The humble who acknowledge their sins will be blessed. Their prayers will be heard because they understand their unworthiness and God's undeserved grace. And when they do receive this grace, they should not boast that they deserve it (1 Corinthians 1:29).

Jesus commended the faith of only two people, both Gentiles. I know I have mentioned them before, but they are worthy of another look. What was it about the faith of these non-Jews that our Lord found commendable? Both individuals exhibited great humility, as well as wisdom.

A Roman centurion requested that Jesus heal his servant. However, he understood that he was not worthy that the Jewish rabbi, Jesus, should come under his roof:

- The centurion replied, "Lord, I do not deserve to have you come under my roof. But just say the word, and my servant will be healed. For I myself am a man under authority, with soldiers under me. I tell this one, 'Go,' and he goes; and that one, 'Come,' and he comes. I say to my servant, 'Do this,' and he does it." When Jesus heard this, he was astonished and said to those following him, "I tell you the truth, I have not found anyone in Israel with such great faith" (Matthew 8:8-10).

The centurion understood two things essential to "great faith." To begin with, he understood that he was unworthy of *anything* from this poorly-clad Man. The centurion was thereby humbling himself before the very people who were required to fear him and his office. The centurion also understood something else about God—that if Jesus was so glorious, He could merely speak a word of healing and the deed would be done.

It was these words of humility and wisdom that had "astonished" and impressed Jesus. This is what "great faith" is all about. When we stop trusting in ourselves and our own worth, we are left with no other choice than to trust in *Christ's* worthiness and all-sufficiency.

Sadly, many of us have learned to trust in the level of our faith and in our own mental abilities to banish doubts. Some of us even believe that we have learned the right techniques to get our prayers heard. However, when we trust in Christ's sufficiency, we realize that our words, our techniques, and our mental states don't really matter:

- We do not know what we ought to pray for, but the Spirit himself intercedes for us with groans that words cannot express. And he who searches our hearts knows the mind of the Spirit, because the Spirit intercedes for the saints in accordance with God's will (Romans 8:26-27).

The truth is that we don't even need to worry about whether we have prayed correctly or not! We serve a glorious, all-sufficient God. Understanding this is freeing. We come to realize that we are completely surrounded by His care. Therefore, God Himself will compensate for any uncertainties and inadequacies we might have about our prayers.

Let us now take a look at how Jesus acknowledged the great faith of another Gentile...

A Canaanite woman asked Jesus to deliver her demon-possessed daughter, but Jesus declined. He reasoned that, since she wasn't a Jew, she was unworthy. However, she was willing to acknowledge her unworthiness, stating that she would be content to eat the crumbs—like a dog—that fell from the table:

- Then Jesus answered, "Woman, you have great faith! Your request is granted." And her daughter was healed from that very hour (Matthew 15:28).

Like the centurion, the Canaanite woman exhibited great understanding, which came from her humility.

How do we tie all this together? Let's try looking at it this way: according to Ezekiel 36:25-26, it is the Lord who circumcises our heart, removing the hard, impenetrable foreskin. With our newly-opened heart, we are enabled to receive the truth about God—through faith—and the truth about ourselves, which in turn makes us humble. Consequently, the great faith of this Gentile woman was associated with humility and the wisdom that comes from humility. That is why Jesus acknowledged her "great faith."

Faith, therefore, represents more than just a change of ideas and beliefs, but also a change of heart towards God. Therefore, it is essential to a relationship with God:

- And without faith it is impossible to please God, because anyone who comes to him must believe that he exists and that he rewards those who earnestly seek him (Hebrews 11:6).

Faith includes belief in the truth—that "he exists and that he rewards those who earnestly seek Him." As we grow in the truth and understanding of God, we grow in faith. As we humble ourselves before God to acknowledge the truths about Him and about ourselves, He will exalt us. When, instead of trusting in God, we believe in ourselves, we will be humbled, and our prayers will not be rewarded.

When we humble ourselves, recognizing our inability to even manage our own lives, we no longer want our own ways, thoughts, or goals. Instead, we seek *Him* first, and He provides everything that we need (Matthew 6:33). When we trust in ourselves and seek our own goals, we have no right to expect to receive anything, no matter how fervent our prayers might be.

Therefore Jesus, in His model prayer, emphasized submission to the will of God:

- "This, then, is how you should pray: 'Our Father in heaven, hallowed be your name, your kingdom come, your will be done on earth as it is in heaven. Give us today our daily bread'" (Matthew 6:9-11).

God's will must take precedence over our own. Only after praying for *His* will should we then pray for our daily bread.

This truth is of utmost importance. Many believe that prayer is about *our* will and getting what *we* want. They cite verses that seem to suggest that Jesus has given us a blank check to get from Him anything that we desire. For proof, they cite this verse:

- "For everyone who asks receives; he who seeks finds; and to him who knocks, the door will be opened. Which of you, if his son asks for bread, will give him a stone? Or if he asks for a fish, will give him a snake? If you, then, though you are evil, know how to give good gifts to your children, how much more will your Father in heaven give good gifts to those who ask him!" (Matthew 7:8-11)

However, when we read these verses along with the next one (7:12), we find that Jesus does not offer us a blank check. His promise contains a *proviso*. We need to live for Him and keep His commandments. After all, we will reap what we sow. We need to embrace God's will to love Him...and our neighbors as ourselves. This is what Jesus taught:

- Jesus replied: "'Love the Lord your God with all your heart and with all your soul and with all your mind.' This is the first and greatest commandment. And the second is like it: 'Love your neighbor as yourself'" (Matthew 22:37-39).

In light of this, we must humble ourselves to do God's will and, once again, obey His two greatest commandments—loving God and loving our neighbors as ourselves. Then, we can expect God to hear us. If we refuse to do this, all bets and promises are off!

Of course, we must always keep in mind that, even when we are obedient, we can never boast about it. And why not? Any good we do is the product of the Spirit, the fruit of His work in us:

- …continue to work out your salvation with fear and trembling, *for it is God who works in you to will and to act according to his good purpose* (Philippians 2:12b-13, emphasis added).

We must always remember that even Jesus' prayers were heard because of His submission to the will of His Father:

- During the days of Jesus' life on earth, he offered up prayers and petitions with loud cries and tears to the one who could save him from death, and he was heard because of his reverent submission (Hebrews 5:7).

Now that our understanding of prayer has been expanded, where does the issue of doubt fit in? James claims that if we doubt, we should not expect to receive anything from the Lord (James 1:6). This is a hard truth for many of us. I will deal with this matter in the next chapter.

Chapter 5

BELIEVING, DOUBTING AND RECEIVING

I was often told that if I wanted God to answer my prayers, I had to believe—without any doubt—that He would answer them. I found this very troubling. How could I not have doubts? I had already experienced a number of unanswered prayers. How then could I *not* doubt that my latest prayer might also go unanswered? Although this teaching was a definite threat to even the little bit of faith that I had, the message of James seemed to be crystal clear that there was to be no room in my prayers for any doubt:

- If any of you lacks wisdom, he should ask God, who gives generously to all without finding fault, and it will be given to him. But when he asks, he must believe and not doubt, because he who doubts is like a wave of the sea, blown and tossed by the wind. That man should not think he will receive anything from the Lord; he is a double-minded man, unstable in all he does (James 1:5-8).

I liked the first verse. It promised that God would generously give me wisdom without censuring me for asking, and I certainly needed wisdom. However, it seemed that the following verses reversed this wonderful promise. I would not be receiving anything from the Lord. After all, I struggled with doubt, and this truth about my life made me both "double-minded" and "unstable."

I knew I couldn't possibly reach God's standards, and so His promise of wisdom was useless to me. And even worse than

44

that, the ongoing existence of my doubts suggested that I might not even be one of His children!

However, as I studied Scripture, I began to see that many of God's servants doubted. Yet God did not abandon them to their doubts. For example, John the Baptist had doubted. He was the one who testified that he had seen the Holy Spirit descend on Jesus. He was the one who had proclaimed that Jesus was "the Lamb of God who takes away the sins of the world." But when this great prophet and evangelist was thrown into prison, he too doubted. He even sent his disciples to Jesus to determine if He was really the Messiah.

The way Jesus responded is so interesting. He did not send the disciples of John back with a reprimand that their leader should simply quit doubting. No way! Instead, the Lord graciously and specifically addressed the Baptist's doubts with good, solid evidence:

- "Go back and report to John what you hear and see: The blind receive sight, the lame walk, those who have leprosy are cured, the deaf hear, the dead are raised, and the good news is preached to the poor" (Matthew 11:4-5).

Jesus was always ready to provide evidence to support the often-failing faith of His disciples. After His crucifixion, they had cloistered themselves in a hideaway. However, Christ Himself—now the risen Lord—passed through the walls of their locked safe-house to encourage His friends *while they were saturated with disbelief*:

- "Why are you troubled, and why do doubts rise in your minds? Look at my hands and my feet. It is I myself! Touch me and see; a ghost does not have flesh and bones, as you see I have" (Luke 24:38-39).

45

The disciples had doubted…and yet they had received!

I was incredibly relieved by this truth, but then I had to wrestle with another problem: how was I to understand James? Perhaps there were different *categories* of doubting… and perhaps James had a more serious form of doubt in mind.

James equates doubting with being "double-minded." Perhaps he had the hypocritical, unrepentant sinner in mind, not the person struggling with honest doubts, like Jesus' disciples.

I found that the Greek word for "double-minded" is used only one other time in Scripture, and that is in the fourth chapter of James:

- Come near to God and he will come near to you. Wash your hands, you sinners, and purify your hearts, you double-minded. Grieve, mourn and wail. Change your laughter to mourning and your joy to gloom. Humble yourselves before the Lord, and he will lift you up (James 4:8-10).

These verses revealed several things about this double-minded person. First of all, he was a "sinner" who needed to repent. He also needed to "Grieve, mourn and wail." Evidently, he hadn't "Come near to God." He seemed to be someone who prayed and used "God-talk," but his heart was far from Him. He would receive nothing from God until he humbled himself by confessing his sins and double-mindedness.

This reminded me of the time when the Lord escorted the prophet Ezekiel on a tour of the Temple, to see the duplicitous secrets of the "seventy elders of the house of Israel":

- He said to me [Ezekiel], "Son of man, have you seen what the elders of the house of Israel are doing in the

darkness, each at the shrine of his own idol? They say,
'The LORD does not see us; the LORD has forsaken
the land'" (Ezekiel 8:12-13).

Outwardly, the elders might have looked pious; but inwardly,
they were living another life. This reminded me of friends who
had also claimed that "the LORD has forsaken the land." They
explained to me that they had prayed about certain things, but
the Lord had not answered them. Since He had not come
through for them, these friends came to the convenient
conclusion that they would now have to take charge of their
own lives, the very thing they had wanted to do all along. They
continued to pray, but now their trust was more in themselves
and not in the Lord.

I began to notice that there were many kinds of doubting.
Surprisingly, I discovered that there were even some kinds of
doubt that were not contrary to faith. As I read the book of
Acts, I found out that the Bereans doubted Paul's message,
and yet their doubt was actually commended:

- Now the Bereans were of more noble character than
  the Thessalonians, for they received the message with
  great eagerness and examined the Scriptures every
  day to see if what Paul said was true (Acts 17:11).

This was very encouraging!

THE SANCTIFIED ROLE OF DOUBT

Biblical prophets and teachers were never to be simply
accepted and believed. Instead, their words and teachings
were to be thoroughly examined or, we might say, doubted:

- Dear friends, do not believe every spirit, but *test the
  spirits* to see whether they are from God, because

many false prophets have gone out into the world (1 John 4:1, emphasis added).

The church at Ephesus was commended for doing this very thing:

- I know your deeds…I know that you cannot tolerate wicked men, that *you have tested those who claim to be apostles but are not*, and have found them false (Revelation 2:2, emphasis added).

It is not easy to be a doubter or tester of the words and ideas of pastors and teachers, but I have found that there is definitely a place for me and for those like me in the Body of Christ. In fact, *everything* is to be doubted and examined for the safeguarding of the church (Deuteronomy 13:1-5; 18:21-22; 1 Thessalonians 5:21).

I began to see that the so-called "faith teachers and preachers," who claim that we Christians need to close down our skeptical, doubting minds in order to receive anything from the Lord, are wrong. God gave us our minds and doubts for a reason—once again—to seek out and then safeguard the truth.

In addition to the beneficial forms of doubting that I have just mentioned, there are other forms of doubting that are a normal part of our growth as we become mature Christians. We must remember that any meaningful growth is painful. For a tree to grow, it must break through its old barriers and defenses, the smooth bark that had once protected the tree. In that process, the tree develops tears and stretch marks associated with the rough bark of older trees. We too must grow by doubting, re-examining, and breaking through our old boundaries—our old ways of thinking.

Believing was a stretch for Jesus' disciples. He would often address them as "Ye of little faith." Over and over again, it seemed as if they were just not "getting it." They would at times try mightily to stretch their faith, but they would mostly fail. On one occasion, they saw Jesus walking on the water towards their boat. In a great display of faith, Peter cried out:

- "Lord, if it's you," Peter replied, "tell me to come to you on the water." "Come," he said. Then Peter got down out of the boat, walked on the water and came toward Jesus. But when he saw the wind, he was afraid and, beginning to sink, cried out, "Lord, save me!" Immediately Jesus reached out his hand and caught him. "You of little faith," he said, "why did you doubt?" And when they climbed into the boat, the wind died down. Then those who were in the boat worshiped him, saying, "Truly you are the Son of God" (Matthew 14:28-33).

Peter's doubt wasn't the result of a lack of commitment. After all, had he not just left the safety of a boat to walk on a storm-tossed sea? Instead, he and the rest of the disciples were not fully convinced of Jesus' divine identity. However, after this incident, they expressed their deeper understanding of who Jesus truly was by their declaration: "Truly you are the Son of God."

We too have a deficient understanding of faith. We wrongly regard it as our personal possession and expect it to be fully amenable to our control and manipulation. We think that faith is about an amount, and then we place our trust in what we deem to be the sufficiency of our *own* faith. We look to ourselves instead of to Christ, our real hope. We become self-centered rather than God-centered.

Jesus encouraged His disciples not to regard the *extent* of their own faith, but the *object* of their faith—God. The smallest measure of faith—a mustard seed's worth—was enough (Luke 17:5-10).

However, like the disciples on the Sea of Galilee, we always need to grow in our understanding of the One in whom we believe (2 Peter 1:2-3; 1 Timothy 4:6; and 1 Peter 4:12). We need to continually learn the truths of our faith and the fact that we will be called upon to endure many painful trials.

There is no escaping this fact of the Christian life. I had tried. I prayed that I would be relieved of all of my painful doubts and the weakness of my faith. However, Christ never answered these prayers. The Lord had another purpose for my weakness and my tendency to doubt everything that came my way. He would use these so-called shortcomings to create His strength in me, according to 2 Corinthians 12:9-10:

- But he said to me, "My grace is sufficient for you, for my power is made perfect in weakness." Therefore I will boast all the more gladly about my weaknesses, so that Christ's power may rest on me. That is why, for Christ's sake, I delight in weaknesses, in insults, in hardships, in persecutions, in difficulties. For when I am weak, then I am strong.

The Lord would build within me a confident knowledge of Him. He faithfully and lovingly coerced me, through the torment of my doubts, to meditate on His Word day and night in hope of finding answers.

When I wasn't able to find a way to reconcile stubborn verses, it felt as if I were drowning. I had banked everything on Scripture. It was as if I had walked out on an ice-covered lake. If that lake was not able to support the weight of my confused life and thinking, I would fall through the ice to my death.

I heard the ice cracking all around me, but it never gave way. In retrospect, I realized that the "ice" had been strengthened and underpinned by God Himself.

- Praise be to the God and Father of our Lord Jesus Christ! In his great mercy he has given us new birth into a living hope through the resurrection of Jesus Christ from the dead, and into an inheritance that can never perish, spoil or fade—kept in heaven for you, *who through faith are shielded by God's power* until the coming of the salvation that is ready to be revealed in the last time (1 Peter 1:3-5, emphasis added).

My faith was a gift from my Savior, and He would safeguard it!

We worry too much about the size of our faith and our control—or lack thereof—over our doubts and thoughts. Once again, we need to remember that we can do nothing without Him (John 15:5). Therefore, we need to *fully* entrust our growth to Him, and actively submit ourselves to the means that He chooses to bring about that growth.

Each and every one of us has within him impediments to the faith that are so deep that only God can uproot them at their foundation. We always try to compensate for our doubts and insecurities with self-trust. But that is the very enemy of trusting in Christ. We love to believe in ourselves, but the futility of this misguided bondage to self-trust must be broken.

Jesus had sent out His disciples. After their return, a father claimed that they had failed to cast out the demon from his son. After Jesus cast it out, His disciples wanted Him to explain the reason for their failure:

- "Why couldn't we drive it out?" He replied, "This kind can come out only by prayer" (Mark 9:28b-29).

What an embarrassing revelation! The disciples had gone out to the mission field without prayer. What would possess them to do such a thing? Evidently, they thought they didn't really need it. And why not? They were convinced that they had everything that the job required. Their faith wasn't truly in Jesus. They had to learn the hard lesson that without Him, they were utterly helpless.

But, let us not forget as well, that their failures and self-doubts were essential components in the process of learning this lesson.

OTHER DOUBTS ARE MORE SERIOUS

There are some doubts that are so extreme that they represent a rejection of the faith.

- The LORD said to Moses, "How long will these people treat me with contempt? How long will they *refuse to believe in me*, in spite of all the miraculous signs I have performed among them?" (Numbers 14:11, emphasis added)

In the story of the Israelites found in the Hebrew Scriptures, doubts were often used as justification for unbelief. When the Israelites absolutely refused to believe and trust in God, they resorted to doubting that He could actually provide for them:

- But they continued to sin against him [despite His many miracles], rebelling in the desert against the Most High. They willfully put God to the test by demanding the food they craved. They spoke against God, saying, "Can God spread a table in the desert?" (Psalm 78:17-19)

Our God is long-suffering, but He has His limits…

- God's anger rose against them; he put to death the sturdiest among them, cutting down the young men of Israel. In spite of all this, they kept on sinning; in spite of his wonders, they did not believe (Psalm 78:31-32).

Therefore, like the Israelites of old, we can see that some people reject the faith simply because they refuse to believe. However, there are some who reject the faith because of disappointment.

Thomas had doubted his brethren's accounts that they had seen the risen Savior. Despite what the disciples had said and discounting all the miracles he had seen and the prophecies of Jesus' rising from the dead that he had heard, Thomas *refused* to believe. Nevertheless, the risen Christ graciously appeared to Thomas to give him the incontrovertible proof that he had demanded. However, Jesus also used this as an occasion to criticize His disciple:

- Then Jesus told him, "Because you have seen me, you have believed; blessed are those who have not seen and yet have believed" (John 20:29).

Jesus is eager to meet His disappointed, doubting, errant sheep right at the point of their deepest need.

However, there are some who remain hardened in their willful doubt and refusal to believe. According to the Apostle John, when we harden our hearts against the faith in this way, we are considered by God to be liars:

- Who is the liar? It is the man who denies that Jesus is the Christ. Such a man is the antichrist—he denies the Father and the Son (1 John 2:22; 5:10).

WHY DON'T WE RECEIVE WHEN WE PRAY?

One reason we don't receive when we pray is willful doubt, whether we call it unbelief or just plain rebellion. Another reason is the harboring of wrong motives, reflecting a defective faith:

- "You do not have, because you do not ask God. When you ask, you do not receive, because you ask with wrong motives, that you may spend what you get on your pleasures. You adulterous people, don't you know that friendship with the world is hatred toward God? Anyone who chooses to be a friend of the world becomes an enemy of God" (James 4:2-4).

Another reason for unanswered prayer is the matter of sin and unbelief. Peter gives us an example of the kind of sin that will block our prayers:

- Husbands, in the same way be considerate as you live with your wives, and treat them with respect as the weaker partner and as heirs with you of the gracious gift of life, so that nothing will hinder your prayers (1 Peter 3:7).

There are many biblical references about how unrepentant sin blocks us from receiving anything from God. However, will unwanted and unintentional doubting actually prevent us from receiving from the Lord? I have tried to argue against this.

We all experience the temptation to sinfully doubt. According to Hebrews 4:15, Jesus was also tempted in every way that we are tempted, and yet He did not sin. Therefore, doubts and temptations, in themselves, are *not* sins. Rather, these particular kinds of temptations can be positively harnessed to propel a deeper, more prayerful investigation of the Word, as we search for answers. Therefore, doubt is not necessarily the problem. Rather, *the way we respond to our doubts* is the real issue.

Some doubts should be dismissed; others, examined. I am naturally a great doubter. Reflexively, I had doubted God's love for me. Such doubt is terribly painful but eventually led me to a great confidence in His love. I also doubted that the Bible was truly God's Word. However, this doubt also led me, as I studied and prayed, to deeply believe in His Word.

In addition, I doubted my interpretation of the Scriptures, as we all must. Perhaps you are wondering why I should say such a thing. But wasn't it Jesus Himself who warned us that we are blind? And, according to Matthew 7:1-5, that we have a log in our eye that must be removed?

Specifically, there are many confusing verses that seem to give us a blank-check to receive anything we might ask for in prayer. To look at just one example, Peter wanted to know how Jesus was able to make a fig tree wither by merely cursing it. Jesus explained:

- "Have faith in God," Jesus answered. "I tell you the truth, if anyone says to this mountain, 'Go, throw yourself into the sea,' *and does not doubt in his heart* but believes that what he says will happen, it will be done for him. Therefore I tell you, *whatever you ask for in prayer*, believe that you have received it, and it will be yours" (Mark 11:22-24, emphasis added).

However, there is only one way that we can confidently "believe that [we] have received it." Our prayer requests must be in accordance with God's will and His Word.

It is so obvious from the rest of the Scriptures that our God does not and will not give us everything we request. James warned that if we are double-minded in our commitment to the

Lord, we should not expect to receive anything from Him (James 1:6-8). Neither should we expect anything if we ask with wrong motives, hoping to spend what we get on our pleasures (James 4:2-3). We know also that there are many other things that can block our prayers, as we saw in 1 Peter 3:7.

Let us remember that even Jesus prayed that His requests be according to God's will:

- Going a little farther, he fell with his face to the ground and prayed, "My Father, if it is possible, may this cup [the crucifixion] be taken from me. Yet not as I will, but as you will" (Matthew 26:39).

Jesus' prayer was not granted. Instead, He confessed that the will of the *Father* had to trump His own will. Therefore, each and every "whatever" that we pray for must also be subordinated to the will of the Father.

There are also some other things that limit the "whatever" promises, but they will have to wait for another chapter.

Chapter 6

THE PRAYER OF FAITH

There exists in the Church today a "theology of blame" that has hurt many people down through the years. One woman shared with me that after her mother died, a friend told her that if she had prayed with more faith, her mother would not have died. Understandably, the woman was devastated.

Where did this "theology of blame" come from? James is often cited:

- Is any one of you sick? He should call the elders of the church to pray over him and anoint him with oil in the name of the Lord. And the prayer offered in faith will make the sick person well; the Lord will raise him up. If he has sinned, he will be forgiven (James 5:14-15).

From these words of the Apostle James, we discover that the Lord has promised to heal the sick through "…prayer offered in faith." But what if the person prayed for is not healed after prayer? Well, there is one thing we know for sure: *the fault lies not with God.* Therefore, there must be something amiss with the one who is praying. Many times, in situations like this, the reason for the unanswered prayer is thought to be a lack of faith.

So, are we interpreting James correctly? Does he in fact give us a *guarantee* that, by carefully following his instruction, every disease will be healed? I don't think so.

Something that would help us immensely as we try to understand this issue is the importance of correct interpretation of Scripture (2 Timothy 2:15). To see how vital this is, let's examine some other verses from the same chapter of James. There, we find the apostle issuing another one of God's promises:

- My brothers, if one of you should wander from the truth and someone should bring him back, remember this: Whoever turns a sinner from the error of his way will save him from death and cover over a multitude of sins (James 5:19-20).

While it is clear that we do have a responsibility to correct a brother "from the error of his way," we simply do NOT have the power to save anyone from death. That power resides only with the Savior.

So then, could it be that James is mistaken? Absolutely not! He clearly believes that it is God who saves us from death. The Lord accomplishes this through His Word, His Good News:

- He chose to give us birth through the word of truth…(James 1:18a).

- Therefore, get rid of all moral filth and the evil that is so prevalent and humbly accept the word planted in you, which can save you (James 1:21).

How then can James make the claim that *believers* can save the wanderer "from death, and cover a multitude of sins"? Easy! James is only writing here about our responsibility to share the Gospel. People need to hear the Good News to be saved, and we do our part in saving "the wanderer from death" by preaching the Gospel!

Correct interpretation of the Bible is of the utmost importance.

Another pillar of this truth is that we should never expect—whenever a Biblical law or principle is mentioned—that every exception or condition is mentioned along with it.

For an example, let's examine one of the Ten Commandments—"Thou shalt not kill"—for an easy-to-see illustration of this essential principle. We would be hard-pressed to find a more cut-and-dried statement of Biblical truth. And yet, there are many exceptions to this rule within the Hebrew Scriptures. In numerous other passages, the taking of life is sanctioned and even authorized in cases dealing with capital punishment, self-defense, and, of course, some wars.

Do these exceptions contradict the *principle* of not killing? No! These exceptions are merely refinements or qualifications of the law. This is something that all laws require. Any lawyer who wants to do a thorough job on a case will not look merely at the law as stated in the Criminal Codebook. He must also examine the many interpretations, exceptions, and applications of the law, which are not all found in that one book.

This also holds true for anyone who wants to rightly interpret Scripture. To do this, it is not enough to examine only the one verse in question. Instead, *all of the verses touching on the subject must be examined.* Furthermore, our investigation should begin with the immediate context and then expand outward to the context and purpose of the entire Bible.

Now let us return once again to James 5:19-20…

When we examine this passage in the light of the rest of the Scriptures, we can properly understand James' statement that "Whoever turns a sinner from the error of his way will save him from death…" We cannot, by any stretch of the imagination, conclude that we, as believers, have the power of salvation. Instead, James is showing us that our responsibility to speak

PRAYER

to those who "wander from the truth" is only one important element in salvation. But it is not the entire story. What about the way that God is leading? What about His will?

Applying this same interpretive principle to the "prayer of faith" in James 5:15, we come to understand that this verse is spotlighting only one aspect of divine healing.

Prayer alone can heal no one, because prayer is only one important element in what we might call the healing "chain."

But there are other links in this chain, chief among them the strategic role played by God Almighty. If we are going to get any of our prayers answered, it is essential that we believe that He is able to heal. However, in the same context, James mentions another critical aspect of healing—the confession of sins.

- Therefore confess your sins to each other and pray for each other so that you may be healed (James 5:16).

The elders of a church can pray with all the fervency in the world, but if there is a refusal to confess sins, there is a very good chance that healing will not take place. It is of the utmost importance that we confess our sins, not just to God the Father, but to each other.

In James 4, we find other conditions necessary for getting answers to our prayers.

James writes that those who are sick and being prayed for should not be friends of the world. According to James 4:4, this would make them enemies of God. Furthermore, those being prayed for should be humble. After all, James 4:6 states that the proud will be opposed by God and not healed. In verse 8 of the same chapter, we find that those being prayed

60

for should also come near to God. That way, He can come near to them with healing in His outstretched hands.

Most important of all, healing depends on the will of God. No amount of faith, faith confessions, or positive affirmations can supersede this truth:

- Now listen, you who say, "Today or tomorrow we will go to this or that city, spend a year there, carry on business and make money." Why, you do not even know what will happen tomorrow. What is your life? You are a mist that appears for a little while and then vanishes. Instead, you ought to say, "If it is the Lord's will, we will live and do this or that." As it is, you boast and brag. All such boasting is evil (James 4:13-16).

Our words and prayers must conform to the will of God. Claiming otherwise is arrogance and self-deception. We need to remember that our lives carry no more authority or power than the mist. Therefore, let us always acknowledge God's supremacy in every area. How wise we would be to take to heart the words of James: "If it is the Lord's will, we will live and do this or that." To go beyond what God has explicitly promised is to boast, and this, as we have just been reminded, is evil.

Meanwhile, the so-called faith preachers teach that we have the same authority as God. In order to prove this unbiblical claim, they invoke a verse that only applies to God:

- As it is written: "I have made you [Abraham] a father of many nations." He is our father in the sight of God, in whom he believed—the God who gives life to the dead and calls things that are not as though they were (Romans 4:17).

Of course, from this verse and others like it, we find that God can indeed call things into existence. He is, after all, God Almighty. However, this verse does not even hint—as these preachers claim—that we believers have this same ability. Instead, once again, let us remember that the Word describes our lives as a mere mist. As John 15:5 states so succinctly, "…apart from me you can do nothing." If we claim otherwise, then we are guilty of the evil boasting about which James warns us so strenuously.

Now, let us apply all of this to the "prayer of faith."

Do we have the authority to claim that a sick man or woman will be healed? No! It might be the will of God to allow a sick person to die. It might be his or her "time." After all, each of the allotted number of our days was written down in God's book before even one of them came to be (Psalm 139:16). Instead, James wisely advises us not to be so certain about the way things will turn out. Once again, he cautions us to say, "If it is the Lord's will…"

In high-definition contrast, faith preachers are quick to declare: "This man will be healed."

So then, back to the issue *du jour*…how is it that James can claim that "the prayer offered in faith will make the sick person well"? If we are to understand this promise in the context of the rest of the book and in light of the teachings of the whole of Scripture, we can understand the promise this way: The prayer offered in faith will make the sick person well *if it is the Lord's will!*

But doesn't James also say, "The prayer of a righteous man is powerful and effective" (James 5:16)? Yes, absolutely. But once again, let's look carefully at the context. In this particular case, James uses Elijah as an example:

- Elijah was a man just like us. He prayed earnestly that it would not rain, and it did not rain on the land for three and a half years (James 5:17).

From verses like this, the faith preachers teach that God's answer depends upon how "earnestly" we pray—that is, the fervency and forcefulness of our praying. By this line of thinking, if we are fervent and in earnest, our prayers will be answered; if not, our prayers will not be answered.

But what was the source of Elijah's fervency? Elijah's fervent prayer had its source in the will of God as directly expressed to him through the Word of God:

- Now Elijah the Tishbite, from Tishbe in Gilead, said to Ahab, "As the LORD, the God of Israel, lives, whom I serve, there will be neither dew nor rain in the next few years except at my word" (1 Kings 17:1).

This boldness and confidence did not come from the will of Elijah, but the will of God. God had revealed it clearly to Elijah, who then faithfully repeated what God had said.

As we examine the whole story, we find that the Lord was directing Elijah throughout the narrative. According to the Lord's own will and impeccable timing, He sent Elijah back to King Ahab:

- After a long time, in the third year, the word of the LORD came to Elijah: "Go and present yourself to Ahab, and I will send rain on the land." So Elijah went to present himself to Ahab. Now the famine was severe in Samaria (1 Kings 18:1-2).

The Lord now had the attention of Israel. Elijah challenged the priests of Baal to call upon their god to consume an offering with fire...IF their god would oblige:

- "Then you call on the name of your god, and I will call on the name of the LORD. The god who answers by fire—he is God" Then all the people said, "What you say is good." Elijah said to the prophets of Baal, "Choose one of the bulls and prepare it first, since there are so many of you. Call on the name of your god, but do not light the fire." So they took the bull given them and prepared it. Then they called on the name of Baal from morning till noon. "O Baal, answer us!" they shouted. But there was no response; no one answered. And they danced around the altar they had made. At noon Elijah began to taunt them. "Shout louder!" he said. "Surely he is a god! Perhaps he is deep in thought, or busy, or traveling. Maybe he is sleeping and must be awakened." So they shouted louder and slashed themselves with swords and spears, as was their custom, until their blood flowed. Midday passed, and they continued their frantic prophesying until the time for the evening sacrifice. But there was no response, no one answered, no one paid attention (1 Kings 18:24-29).

When Elijah prayed, the bull for the sacrifice was immediately incinerated. There were no hours of waiting and screaming out to a fabricated, deaf, imaginary god. How could Elijah be so bold? Simply this: he knew that he was operating *according to the will and Word of God*, and not on his own:

- At the time of sacrifice, the prophet Elijah stepped forward and prayed: "O LORD, God of Abraham, Isaac and Israel, let it be known today that you are God in Israel and that I am your servant and have done all these things *at your command*" (1 Kings 18:36, emphasis added).

Elijah's confidence did not originate from his faith in prayer or from a faith in his own faith. Rather, he was confident because of his faith in the God whom he served. He knew God's Word, and that was what he banked on. Elijah was not victorious over the priests of Baal through a formless, substance-less prayer of faith, but through his confidence in the very words and will of God.

Now that I know what the Bible says about faith, my prayers are different. When I pray that He will make me more Christ-like, or when I pray that He will build His church, I pray with confidence. I know from His Word that this is what He has promised to do. However, when I pray for someone to be healed, I am confident that God is more than able to heal a multitude, but I also know that healing as we think of it might not be His will for everyone.

Elijah was confident *only* when he had a clear command from his God.

Ironically, following the great victory over the prophets of Baal, Elijah fled in fear from Jezebel. Why did he flee? Could it be that Elijah ran because he did not know the specific will of God in his new set of circumstances?

I am not trying to minimize prayer by my comments. Instead, I want to restore this essential element of the Christian life to its proper glory, alongside the will of God.

In 1976, the Christian historian, J. Edwin Orr, preached about the importance of prayer:

> Dr. A. T. Pierson once said, 'There has never been a spiritual awakening in any country or locality that did not begin in united prayer.' Let me recount what God has done through concerted, united, sustained prayer.
>
> Not many people realize that in the wake of the American Revolution there was a moral slump.

Drunkenness became epidemic. Out of a population of five million, 300,000 were confirmed drunkards; they were burying fifteen thousand of them each year. Profanity was of the most shocking kind. For the first time in the history of the American settlement, women were afraid to go out at night for fear of assault. Bank robberies were a daily occurrence.

What about the churches? The Methodists were losing more members than they were gaining. The Baptists said that they had their most wintry season. The Presbyterians in general assembly deplored the nation's ungodliness. In a typical Congregational church, the Rev. Samuel Shepherd of Lenox, Massachusetts, in sixteen years had not taken one young person into fellowship. The Lutherans were so languishing that they discussed uniting with Episcopalians who were even worse off. The Protestant Episcopal Bishop of New York, Bishop Samuel Provost, quit functioning; he had confirmed no one for so long that he decided he was out of work, so he took up other employment.

The Chief Justice of the United States, John Marshall, wrote to the Bishop of Virginia, James Madison, that the Church 'was too far gone ever to be redeemed.' Voltaire averred and Tom Paine echoed, 'Christianity will be forgotten in thirty years.

Let's take a look at what was happening at the liberal arts colleges at that time.

A poll taken at Harvard had discovered not one believer in the whole student body. They took a poll at Princeton, a much more evangelical place, where they discovered only two believers in the student body, and only five that did not belong to the filthy speech movement of that day. Students rioted. They held a mock communion at Williams College, and they put on anti-Christian plays at Dartmouth. They burned down Nassau Hall at Princeton. They forced the resignation of the president of Harvard. They took a Bible out of a local Presbyterian church in New Jersey and burned it in a public bonfire. Christians were so few on campus in the 1790's that they met in secret, like communist cells, and kept their minutes in code so that no one would know.

How did the situation change? It came through a concert of prayer.

<https://prayforrevival.wordpress.com/category/j-edwin-orr/>.

And what was the result of this fervent prayer? The Second Great Revival that transformed the nation! Orr concluded that these prayers were only effectual because they were consistent with the will and providence of God.

Let us pray accordingly.

Chapter 7

PRAYERS THAT PLEASE GOD

Which prayers does God hear and answer? Which prayers please Him? Thankfully, the Bible has a consistent response to these age-old questions. If we take a good look at the way Solomon addressed the Lord at the consecration of the Temple, we will find a wonderfully God-centered prayer. Here is a representative segment:

- "When they [Israel] sin against you [God]—for there is no one who does not sin—and you become angry with them and give them over to the enemy, who takes them captive to a land far away or near; and if they have a change of heart in the land where they are held captive, and repent and plead with you in the land of their captivity and say, 'We have sinned, we have done wrong and acted wickedly'; and if they turn back to you with all their heart and soul in the land of their captivity where they were taken, and pray toward the land you gave their fathers, toward the city you have chosen and toward the temple I have built for your Name; then from heaven, your dwelling place, hear their prayer and their pleas, and uphold their cause. And forgive your people, who have sinned against you" (2 Chronicles 6:36-39).

In just a few short verses, Solomon touched on all the key areas of prayer—sin, righteousness, justice, confession, repentance, forgiveness, and restoration. This is all well and good, but what about the ultimate litmus test? What did God think of Solomon's prayer? Evidently, He was pleased. According to 2 Chronicles 7:1, fire came down from heaven to consume Solomon's offering, indicating that God had received and accepted his prayer.

In addition, God responded with these familiar and beloved words:

- [The] LORD appeared to him at night and said: "I have heard your prayer and have chosen this place for myself as a temple for sacrifices...if my people, who are called by my name, will humble themselves and pray and seek my face and turn from their wicked ways, then will I hear from heaven and will forgive their sin and will heal their land" (2 Chronicles 7:12, 14).

What did it mean for Israel to "humble themselves"? Jesus told a parable about two people who entered the Temple to pray. The Pharisee was self-righteous and looked down on everyone else. The tax-collector was despised and held in contempt by all. The Pharisee's prayer was about himself and his assumed worthiness before God. The tax-collector could only cry out, "Have mercy on me, a sinner."

And yet, it was the tax-collector, humbling himself and confessing his unworthiness, who ended up receiving forgiveness. Jesus explained:

- "I tell you that this man, rather than the other, went home justified before God. For everyone who exalts himself will be humbled, and he who humbles himself will be exalted" (Luke 18:14).

However, according to the faith or prosperity preachers—sometimes referred to as the "name-it-and-claim-it preachers"—humility has nothing to do with receiving from God. Instead, demanding our rights is the key.

Pat Robertson once stated:

- "Most people ask God for a miracle but many omit a key requirement—the spoken word. God has given us authority over disease, over demons, over sickness, over storms, over finances. We are to declare that authority in Jesus' name...*We are to command the money to come to us*" (Horton, Michael. The Agony of Deceit. Chicago, Ill.: Moody Press, 1992: 128, emphasis added).

Actually, the clear teaching of the Bible declares that everything God gives us is the outworking of His unmerited favor. *God never owes us anything!*

- Who has ever given to God, that God should repay him? For from him and through him and to him are all things. To him be the glory forever! (Romans 11:35-36)

Since, according to James 1:17, all good things come from God, we are always beholden to Him. According to Jesus in Luke 17:10, even if we do everything that we are supposed to do, we are to consider ourselves unworthy servants. And yet the prosperity preachers have the audacity to claim that we are so worthy that we have the right "...to command the money to come to us."

Commanding God is something that we never find in Scripture. Perhaps the closest thing to this was the hubris of Simon the magician, who wanted to pay God for a supernatural gift. The Apostle Peter was horrified by such an arrogant suggestion:

- Peter answered, "May your money perish with you, because you thought you could buy the gift of God with money! You have no part or share in this ministry, because your heart is not right before God. Repent of this wickedness and pray to the Lord. Perhaps he will forgive you for having such a thought in your heart. For I see that you are full of bitterness and captive to sin" (Acts 8:20-23).

To think that we might receive something from God through either our money or good deeds shows that our minds are "captive to sin" and still tainted with darkness. In contrast, Solomon's prayer reflected a mature understanding that *everything* comes to us through the mercy of God.

Prior to the experiences that I mentioned from 2 Chronicles, Solomon had prayed for wisdom:

- "Now, O LORD my God, you have made your servant king in place of my father David. But I am only a little child and do not know how to carry out my duties. Your servant is here among the people you have chosen, a great people, too numerous to count or number. So give your servant a discerning heart to govern your people and to distinguish between right and wrong. For who is able to govern this great people of yours?" The Lord was pleased that Solomon had asked for this (1 Kings 3:7-10).

The Lord was pleased that Solomon hadn't asked for wealth and power. Instead, he asked for wisdom to govern the beloved people of God. And let us not overlook the fact that Solomon did not *command* wisdom to come to him. In fact, no righteous person in the Bible ever presumed to do such a thing.

Certainly King David never had such expectations, and Solomon had learned well from his father. David knew how to pray humbly to God. Confessing that he deserved nothing from God but punishment, David found the blessing of the Lord through confession:

- Blessed is he whose transgressions are forgiven, whose sins are covered. Blessed is the man whose sin the LORD does not count against him and in whose spirit is no deceit. When I kept silent, my bones wasted away through my groaning all day long. For day and night your hand was heavy upon me; my strength was sapped as in the heat of summer. Then I acknowledged my sin to you and did not cover up my iniquity. I said, "I will confess my transgressions to the LORD"—and you forgave the guilt of my sin" (Psalm 32:1-5).

David understood that blessedness was a matter of receiving the grace of God through the humble confession of his sins—not from claiming things that he did not deserve.

In stark contrast, prosperity preachers claim that we can establish heavenly merit through good deeds and then demand payment. Joyce Meyers claimed:

- "It says in Romans 4:17 that...we have a God who gives life to the dead and He calls things that be not as though they already existed...If there's something in your way, speak it...When I talked with Dr. Roberts today and we talked about this seed-faith thing, he said...when you give you get a receipt in heaven that when you have a need you can then go with your receipt and say "You see, God, I have got my receipt from my sowing and now I have a need and I'm cashing in my receipt'" (Hunter, Robert, "Christianity Still in Crisis?" Christian Research Journal 30:3 (2007).

Meyers is right about one thing. God will answer us according to our deeds or righteousness. However, this doesn't mean that God *owes* us anything—Romans 11:35—or that we have a heavenly bank account in the black from which we have the right to draw. Rather, if we were to draw from God what we rightfully deserve, we would end up receiving nothing but condemnation!

It is by the mercy of God *alone* that we receive anything good from Him. Jesus Himself taught that we do not even deserve a "thank you" from God. Instead, according to Luke 17:6-10, we are to consider ourselves as unworthy servants, not deserving anything from Him.

Then, how do we understand the fact that God blesses us according to our obedience if we are unworthy servants? We must remember from Philippians 2:12-13 that *His blessing is the fruit that He produces in us through our obedience!*

The apostle Paul confessed that he could not take credit for any of his labors, let alone make demands on God because of his supposed heavenly account:

- But by the grace of God I am what I am, and his grace to me was not without effect. No, I worked harder than all of them—yet not I, but the grace of God that was with me (1 Corinthians 15:10).

Therefore, it is plain to see that it is God who deserves the credit, even for our labors. Sound confusing? Well, it is! God produces the fruit and yet, we must still take responsibility for what we do. Can we understand this fully? No!

What the Bible is clear about is the fact that, if we deserve anything from God, it is death:

- For the wages of sin is death, but the gift of God is eternal life in Christ Jesus our Lord (Romans 6:23).

While it is true that our heavenly account will always be in the red, our Savior has rescued us and given us life.

Returning once again to Joyce Meyers, we need to point out that she is mistaken about Romans 4:17 in yet another way, as well. Yes, *God* has the power to call things into existence from nothing. However, there is nothing in this verse to suggest that *we* have such a power. Claiming that we do places us on the same level as God. And this represents an outright denial of the revelation of God found in His word.

Instead, the prayers that move God are characterized by a humble brokenness—the acknowledgement that any blessing we receive comes to us because of the mercy of God.

King Hezekiah had been a good king. And yet, because of his success and wealth, he had become proud and had distanced himself from God. Therefore, God struck him down with a fatal disease. However, Hezekiah did not pray in the manner that some of the faith preachers might have recommended. He did not say: "I am healthy and will live to be 100!" Instead, according to Isaiah 38:3, he "wept bitterly." And God granted his prayer for life.

As a result, Hezekiah thanked God:

- "I waited patiently till dawn, but like a lion he [God] broke all my bones; day and night you made an end of me. I cried like a swift or thrush, I moaned like a mourning dove. My eyes grew weak as I looked to the heavens. I am troubled; O Lord, come to my aid! But what can I say? He has spoken to me, and he himself has done this. I will walk humbly all my years because of this anguish of my soul. Lord, by such things men live; and my spirit finds life in them too. You restored me to health and let me live. Surely it was for my benefit that I suffered such anguish. In your love you kept me from the pit of destruction; you have put all my sins behind your back" (Isaiah 38:13-17).

Hezekiah's illness produced humility. He acknowledged that God's ways are just and that God, in His mercy, had struck His servant down.

In contrast to this display of appropriate humility, TV megachurch pastor Joel Osteen claims that our words have "enormous creative power":

- "Our words are vital in bringing our dreams to pass. It's not enough to simply see it by faith or in your imagination. You have to begin speaking words of faith over your life. Your words have enormous creative power. The moment you speak something out, you give birth to it...Just look in the mirror and say 'I am strong, I am healthy. I'm rising to new levels, I'm excited about my future.' When you say that, it may not be true. You may not be very healthy today, or maybe you don't have a lot of things to look forward to, but Scripture tells us in Romans [4:17] we have to call the things that are not as if they already were" (Hunter, Robert, "Christianity Still in Crisis?" Christian Research Journal 30:3 (2007).

Scripture gives us absolutely no indication that we have such power. Rather, God wants truth in our inmost being (Psalm 51:6). We have no right or authorization to play fast and loose with the truth. After all, *all truth is God's truth*. Consequently, we are not free to manipulate, re-configure or re-imagine the situations we are in as we so choose.

Let us examine the way that James chastens those who speak with such arrogance. In this particular case, he is referring to those who claim that they will make a financial killing:

- Instead, you ought to say, "If it is the Lord's will, we will live and do this or that." As it is, you boast and brag. All such boasting is evil (James 4:15-16).

Our words must conform to God's reality and not to our imaginations and dreams.

Claiming that we can shape reality with our words is boasting. Instead, we need to acknowledge that it is all about "the Lord's will." In the same passage of verses as those mentioned above, James claims that we need to realize that we are no more than "...a mist that appears for a little while and then vanishes" (James 4:14b). We are incapable of succeeding at anything apart from God.

King Manasseh of Judah was the worst of the worst. He reigned for 55 years in Jerusalem and bathed the city with the blood of the righteous. Scripture informs us that he was worse than the Canaanites. However, Manasseh was captured by the Assyrians and thrown into jail. There, he humbled himself in prayer before the God he had hated:

- In his distress he sought the favor of the LORD his God and humbled himself greatly before the God of his fathers. And when he prayed to him, the LORD was moved by his entreaty and listened to his plea; so he brought him back to Jerusalem and to his kingdom. Then Manasseh knew that the LORD is God (2 Chronicles 33:12-13).

Amazingly, God restored Manasseh to the throne! Had Joel Osteen counseled Manasseh in prison, he more than likely would have advised him like this:

- "The moment you speak something out, you give birth to it...Just look in the mirror and say 'I am strong, I am healthy. I'm rising to new levels, I'm excited about my future.'"

However, the rationale for such an assertion, founded on a total disregard for the truth of the situation, cannot be found in Scripture. We can be certain that God would not have responded favorably to such a prayer.

THE CHAPTER 9 PRAYERS OF THE HEBREW BIBLE

All of the great prayers of the Bible are characterized by humility—the acknowledgement of sin and the overwhelming need for mercy. Now, let us examine some of those prayers in the three great "Chapter Nine" prayers of the Hebrew Scriptures.

In each of these prayers—all found in Chapter Nine of the books of Ezra, Nehemiah and Daniel, respectively—there is found a confession of sin. Concurrent with that confession is a recognition that Israel deserved nothing from God but judgment.

Ezra's prayer starts this way:

- "O my God, I am too ashamed and disgraced to lift up my face to you, my God, because our sins are higher than our heads and our guilt has reached to the heavens" (Ezra 9:6).

Far be it from Ezra to minimize the weightiness of Israel's sins or to make light of them. If sin is not trivial in God's eyes, then it must not be so in ours. We must treat sin with the seriousness with which our Lord regards it. The sins we commit are so weighty that only the shed blood of the Son of God could atone for them. Therefore, Ezra would never have said anything like this: "OK God, we sinned…but what do You expect of us mere mortals living in this fallen world?"

In contrast with Ezra, the modern-day "mystics" seem to have an inadequate understanding of sin and its utter offense to God. They believe that they can do an end-run around God's concerns—repentance, confession, humility, and righteousness—in favor of gimmicks and methods which they claim will usher them into the presence of God.

The late Catholic priest and mystic, Henry Nouwen, reduces prayer to the repetition of a single word:

- The quiet repetition of a single word can help us to descend with the mind into the heart...This way of simple prayer...opens us to God's active presence (Nouwen, Henri. The Way of the Heart. New York: Seabury Press, 1981: 81).

Nouwen, in lock-step with many other mystics, believes that the mind is an impediment to experiencing God or receiving anything from Him. Therefore, many of the techniques of the mystics—like the repetition of one word—are designed to quiet the mind. However, these practices find absolutely no sanction within Scripture.

In contrast with the mystics who want to silence the mind and its understanding, the counsel we find in the Bible assures us that understanding is key:

- Grace and peace be yours in abundance through the knowledge of God and of Jesus our Lord. His divine power has given us everything we need for life and godliness through our knowledge of him who called us by his own glory and goodness. Through these he has given us his very great and precious promises, so that through them you may participate in the divine nature and escape the corruption in the world caused by evil desires (2 Peter 1:2-4).

To say that there is an abundance of blessings given to us through the knowledge of God is an understatement. To turn off the mind is to turn off these blessings from our Lord. Besides, Scripture tells us that in spiritual matters, we should not venture beyond what is written (1 Corinthians 4:6-7; Isaiah 8:20). In fact, we require no further instructions other than Scripture:

- All Scripture is God-breathed and is useful for teaching, rebuking, correcting and training in righteousness, so that the man of God may be thoroughly equipped for every good work (2 Timothy 3:16-17).

Nouwen's method is not only *non*-Scriptural; it is *anti*-Scriptural. The Lord Jesus gave explicit instructions about this issue:

- "And when you pray, do not keep on babbling like pagans, for they think they will be heard because of their many words" (Matthew 6:7).

In The Signature of Jesus, Brennan Manning offers the same misguided and erroneous suggestion as Nouwen:

- "The first step in faith is to stop thinking about God in prayer...Contemplative spirituality tends to emphasize the need for a change in consciousness...we must come to see reality differently...Choosing a single, sacred word...repeat the sacred word inwardly, slowly, and often...Enter into the great silence of God. Alone in that silence, the noise within will subside and the Voice of Love will be heard" (Yungen, Ray. A Time of Departing. Eureka, MT: Lighthouse Trails Pub., 2002: 83).

One question we must ask ourselves here is this: How does Manning know whose "voice" he has encountered? By encouraging us to "stop thinking about God," he has cut all ties with Scripture. In both Psalm 1 and Joshua 1:8, we are instructed to meditate on God day and night. Manning has rejected God's priorities and has embarked on his own spiritual quest into the un-mapped, uncertain world of mysticism.

Once again, what is Manning hearing? What is he experiencing? Where is he going? He has no compass or GPS. What then guides him? Perhaps it is his own baseless confidence that he has the intelligence to sort out the shadowy beings he might meet on his journey!

In contrast, the elders under Nehemiah had absolutely no confidence that they could connect with God through their own techniques. Instead, they prayed in a way that accorded with God's truth.

To begin with, they "confessed their sins and the wickedness of their fathers" (Nehemiah 9:2). This was followed by a long segment of praise to God for His faithfulness (Nehemiah 9:5-15). Then, the elders recounted the contrasting historical unfaithfulness of Israel:

- "But they, our forefathers, became arrogant and stiff-necked, and did not obey your commands. They refused to listen and failed to remember the miracles you performed among them. They became stiff-necked and in their rebellion appointed a leader in order to return to their slavery" (Nehemiah 9:16-17).

Years later, Israel returned to their sinful ways. However, Nehemiah made absolutely no attempt to justify the sins of Israel and offered no suggestion that perhaps God had been unduly harsh with His people. In the view of both Ezra and Nehemiah, God had been perfectly just in His actions, even though Israel had endured extreme hardship at His hands.

How was it that both of these men could retain such a view when Israel had suffered so greatly? Ezra and Nehemiah had no doubt that the sins of Israel deserved even worse!

Today, we lack a biblical awareness of the seriousness of our sins and the far-reaching extent of our guilt. We tend to trivialize our sins with rationalizations:

- "Well, God knows my heart. He knows that I am trying as hard as I can."
- "God is love, and so He doesn't want us to feel guilty."
- "God knows that I've been through a lot."
- "I'm more spiritual than most people."
- "I am a good person, and people like me!"
- "No one is perfect."
- "Well, this is a fallen world! What can God expect of us?"

Of course, if we choose to downplay our sin like this, we will also have little respect, taste or understanding for the righteousness and judgments of God. Instead, we might regard Him as slightly tyrannical. Is it any wonder, then, that those who think this way cannot feel intimate with a God they regard as a tyrant?

When we minimize our sins, we also minimize God's forgiveness and the massive price He paid for us on the Cross. With such a skewed mind-set, how grateful would we be to God? How thankful would we be for His multiple blessings? Instead, we would feel as if we were *deserving* of His mercy.

And then we must ask ourselves the question: will God continue to pour out His blessings to those who are ungrateful—to those who have the gall to believe that they are *entitled* to His kindness?

The mystics lack any sense of the enormity of our sins. Once again, they believe that we can come into the presence of God through the practice of various gimmicks. Mystic Tony Campolo writes:

- "A theology of mysticism provides some hope for common ground between Christianity and Islam. Both religions have within their histories examples of ecstatic union with God...Could they have encountered the same God we do in our Christian mysticism?" (Oakland, Roger. Faith Undone. Eureka, MT: Lighthouse Trails Pub., 2002:108)

According to Campolo, we can *all* plug into God through mystical techniques and experiences, irrespective of faith in Christ. He claims that he has been able to achieve intimacy with Christ through "centering prayer" (Ibid, 113)—the repetition of the name of Jesus. However, he seems to be suggesting that Muslims and—by logical extension, others— may also be able to achieve this same intimacy with Christ through the use of similar mystical techniques.

This raises several questions: What is an "ecstatic union with God?" The Bible makes no mention of such a thing. The biblical silence is suspicious, especially in light of the fact that Scripture claims to provide everything that we need for a relationship with God.

Furthermore, if mysticism is the means by which the world will become unified and at peace—as Campolo and others are suggesting—should we not expect that Scripture might have something to say about it?

If anyone had experienced an "ecstatic union with God," it was Jesus on the Mount of Transfiguration. And, what perfect timing for a teachable moment when Jesus could introduce a marvelous new mystical method. However, instead of teaching

His disciples about how they too could have such an experience, He instructed them not to tell anyone about what they had seen! (Matthew 17:11)

Moses also had a fantastic mountain-top experience. Even his countenance had been transformed—his face was glowing with radiant light. However, instead of telling the Israelites about how they too could experience God in this way, he shared with them "all the commands the LORD had given him on Mt. Sinai" (Exodus 34:32).

The words of God trump any kind of ecstatic experience we might have. Instead, God's concern is that His children would simply abide in His Word and not in the hope of having some sort of blissful divine encounter.

Tony Campolo fails to understand that there can be a steep price to be paid for genuine experiences and encounters. God had taken Paul on a journey to heaven. However, lest he become proud about what he had learned and experienced, God chastened him severely. Paul writes that he was even given "...a thorn in my flesh, a messenger of Satan, to torment me" (2 Corinthians 12:7).

It is of the utmost importance for us to realize that each one of these transformative experiences had been the product, not of any *human* manipulation, but by the initiative of *God*. In fact, the idea that we humans can somehow coerce or engineer an "ecstatic union with God" is sheer arrogance.

Let us consider something else at this juncture: do the mystics really encounter God through their techniques? What assurance do they have that they aren't really plugging into something malevolent?

The mystic Richard Foster claims...

- …that practitioners must use caution. He admits that in contemplative prayer "we are entering deeply into the spiritual realm" and that sometimes it is not the realm of God even though it is "supernatural." He admits there are spiritual beings and that a prayer of protection should be said beforehand—something to the effect of "All dark and evil spirits must now leave" (Oakland, Roger. <u>Faith Undone</u>. Eureka, MT: Lighthouse Trails Pub., 2002:99).

Foster is presumptuous if he thinks that a mere "prayer of protection" will suffice. Considering these very real spiritual threats, he should be asking if he has taken the wrong path, an unbiblical one—one that has taken him outside God's protective hand! In view of the fact that the Devil poses as an agent of light (2 Corinthians 11:14), what guarantee does Foster have that he has not been deceived?

This leads us to the next question: "Can people of other religions employ mystical techniques to experience God?" For one thing, it is important for us to remember that God is the last Person that the unredeemed want to experience. Naturally-speaking, we hate God (Romans 8:6-7) and cannot stand His presence:

- This is the verdict: Light has come into the world, but men loved darkness instead of light because their deeds were evil. Everyone who does evil hates the light, and will not come into the light for fear that his deeds will be exposed (John 3:19-20).

Even the children of Israel could not tolerate the Lord's presence:

- When the people saw the thunder and lightning and heard the trumpet and saw the mountain in smoke, they trembled with fear. They stayed at a distance and said to Moses, "Speak to us yourself and we will listen. But do not have God speak to us or we will die" (Exodus 20:18-19).

The last thing the Israelites wanted was a more intimate encounter with God!

Surprisingly, we find that God was *pleased* that Israel had this mind-set and, therefore, would not try to pursue a mystical union with Him:

- "I have heard what this people said to you [Moses]. Everything they said was good" (Deuteronomy 5:28b).

Now, from the very next sentence, let us see what God's priorities for the Israelites were:

- "Oh, that their hearts would be inclined to fear me and keep all my commands always, so that it might go well with them and their children forever!" (Deuteronomy 5:29)

From these and many other verses like them, it is abundantly clear that, more than mystical union with Him, God wanted His people to obey His laws and commands.

Before the monumental accomplishment of the cross, the Father had no desire to be in Israel's presence. He explained that He might destroy them if He were to come near:

- "I will send an angel before you and drive out the Canaanites, Amorites, Hittites, Perizzites, Hivites and Jebusites. Go up to the land flowing with milk and honey. But I will not go with you, because you are a stiff-necked people and I might destroy you on the way" (Exodus 33:2-3).

Campolo suggests that Muslims might also be experiencing God, once again, through some sort of ecstatic union with Him. However, from what the Scriptures plainly teach, if anyone were to experience God apart from faith in Christ, he or she would be experiencing His wrath:

- The wrath of God is being revealed from heaven against all the godlessness and wickedness of men who suppress the truth by their wickedness (Romans 1:18).

It is only through faith in Jesus that we have been redeemed and rescued from the wrath of God. It is only through Him that we can enter boldly into His presence:

- Therefore, brothers, since we have confidence to enter the Most Holy Place by the blood of Jesus, by a new and living way opened for us through the curtain, that is, his body, and since we have a great priest over the house of God, let us draw near to God with a sincere heart in full assurance of faith, having our hearts sprinkled to cleanse us from a guilty conscience and having our bodies washed with pure water (Hebrews 10:19-22).

Finally, mysticism would not be quite so offensive if it only claimed to influence *our* personal experience. However, it also claims to influence *God*!

Here is what Tony Campolo has to say about this:

- "The constant repetition of his name clears my head of everything but the awareness of his presence. By driving back all other concerns, I am able to create what the ancient Celtic Christians called "the thin place." The thin place is that spiritual condition wherein the separation between the self and God becomes so thin that *God is able to break through and envelope the soul*" (Oakland, Roger. <u>Faith Undone</u>. Eureka, MT: Lighthouse Trails Pub., 2002:114, emphasis added).

By careful examination of such faulty thinking, we can see that the god of the mystic is not omnipotent. *He requires our help through the use of our techniques.* In addition, the mystic shows little appreciation for the totally impassible gulf between us and God. There is no "thin place." Outside of Christ, there is an impermeable wall separating us from God.

The convoluted thinking of the mystics is a serious problem for many reasons. When we minimize sin and its life-crippling effects, we minimize grace and our dire need for it.

The prophet Daniel certainly did not feel this way. Here is how he prayed:

- "O Lord, the great and awesome God, who keeps his covenant of love with all who love him and obey his commands, we have sinned and done wrong. We have been wicked and have rebelled; we have turned away from your commands and laws. We have not listened to your servants the prophets, who spoke in your name to our kings, our princes and our fathers, and to all the people of the land. Lord, you are righteous, but this day we are covered with shame— the men of Judah and people of Jerusalem and all Israel, both near and far, in all the countries where you have scattered us because of our unfaithfulness to you. O Lord, we and our kings, our princes and our fathers are covered with shame because we have sinned against you. The Lord our God is merciful and forgiving, even though we have rebelled against him; we have not obeyed the Lord our God or kept the

laws he gave us through his servants the prophets"
(Daniel 9:4-10).

Is God pleased with such prayers? Evidently! While Daniel
was still praying, the archangel Gabriel appeared and
informed him:

- "As soon as you began to pray, an answer was
  given, which I have come to tell you, for you are
  highly esteemed" (Daniel 9:23).

Why was Daniel "highly esteemed?" Well, think about it this
way: have you ever tried to communicate with someone who
thought he had the intelligence of an Einstein? It is hard to
relate to people who have rejected our shared reality in favor
of their own delusions. By rejecting reality, they have rejected
the common ground so necessary for any meaningful
relationship. Even simple conversation is difficult. People like
this are in a different world and require that you affirm their
world in order to enter it.

The mystic also inhabits a different world. He believes that the
only thing that separates him from God is the proper use of his
mystical techniques. According to this way of thinking, once
one applies these methods, "God is able to break through and
envelope the soul."

Poor God! He so badly wants mystical union with us, but such
a union is impossible unless certain conditions are met. The
mystics seem to be saying that God needs our help to break
through. Then, and only then, can such an ecstatic union be
experienced.

Instead, Jesus often warned us against such self-exalting
beliefs:

- "I tell you that...everyone who exalts himself will be humbled, and he who humbles himself will be exalted" (Luke 18:14).

And just what does it mean to humble ourselves? Referring once again to the parable that Jesus shared in Luke 18, the Lord gave us a most telling example of humility. The man who was humble was being totally honest with God and freely admitted that he was indeed a sinner:

- "But the tax collector stood at a distance. He would not even look up to heaven, but beat his breast and said, 'God, have mercy on me, a sinner'" (Luke 18:13).

As far as a genuine relationship with God is concerned, so-called spiritual techniques and other gimmicks will never be able to replace the genuine, humble confession of sins... accompanied by our desperate pleas for the mercy of God.

CONCLUSION

Prayer is a hot topic. It has the audacity to lay claim to God and how He disburses His favors. And of course, everyone wants to think that they have the ear of God.

PRAYER: Confronting the Confusion makes a bold claim. It claims to know what moves God and what opens His hand. As the author of this book, I want to know that I got it right and that I wasn't misleading anyone, not even in the slightest way.

Writing about God, in general, is a bold thing to do. It is also scary, as it should be. Let's take another look at how God had been angry at Job's three friends:

- After the LORD had spoken these words to Job, the LORD said to Eliphaz the Temanite: "My anger burns against you and against your two friends, for you have not spoken of me what is right, as my servant Job has" (Job 42:7).

I am confident of God's mercy. Nevertheless, because it is such a serious thing, I never want to speak incorrectly about Him. If, according to Acts 20:32, it is His truth that builds us up, then it is surely a distortion of His truth that tears us down (1 Timothy 4:1-3).

Have I spoken wrongly about Him? This is a question I am always asking myself. Have I narrowed the broadness of His Word and His will into my narrow theology? Have I been conforming to His Word, or have I been making it conform to my own understanding?

These are questions for which I have answers, but not absolute certainty. Maybe this is how it should be, for this is the state of mind that leads me again and again to prayer and

dependence on Him. Perhaps this is where we should all be—
eternally on our knees, expressing our needs:

- Do not be anxious about anything, but in everything by
  prayer and supplication with thanksgiving let your
  requests be made known to God. And the peace of
  God, which surpasses all understanding, will guard your
  hearts and your minds in Christ Jesus (Philippians 4:6-
  7).

I do not feel anxious about this book. He has given it to me,
and I have given it back to Him. It is His! May He use it for His
glory's sake.

Made in the USA
Middletown, DE
31 March 2019